A Doctrine On
The Beginning Of
Christian Life

VOLUME I

DR. JOHN THOMAS WYLIE

authorHOUSE®

AuthorHouse™
1663 Liberty Drive
Bloomington, IN 47403
www.authorhouse.com
Phone: 1 (800) 839-8640

Published by AuthorHouse 12/13/2019

ISBN: 978-1-7283-3975-7 (sc)
ISBN: 978-1-7283-3974-0 (e)

Print information available on the last page.

Contents

Introduction

IN THIS PUBLICATION, "A Doctrine On The Beginning Of The Christian Faith," It points to the fact that God is working out through Jesus Christ and his Church a redemptive program on the planet. Redemption is to be the goal and peak of creation. There is nothing more profound in the mind and purpose behind God than his plan to redeem. God works out his redemption regardless of the restricting powers on the earth.

The Bible says, "With wicked hands men crucified him, in doing so they carried out what was in the determinate counsel and foreknowledge of God" (Acts 2:23 KJV). Jesus was crucified on our behalf. This is his redemptive work as it works itself out in human experience.

What is becoming a Christian? What sort of a transaction is it? What do we mean by salvation? How is a man saved?

These questions strike a chord when we think about them from the point of view of involvement and life. Is salvation something that takes place all at once or is it a continuous process?

"The Son of man came to seek and to save that which was lost" (Luke 19:10 ASV). Faithful is the saying, and worthy of all acceptation, that Christ Jesus came into the world to save sinners" (I Timothy 1:15 ASV).

"For God so loved the world, that he gave his only begotten Son, that whosoever believeth in him should not perish, but have everlasting life" (John 3:16 KJV). "For God sent not his Son into the world to condemn the world; but that the world through him might be saved" (John 3:17 KJV).

"He that believeth on him is not condemned; but he that believeth not is condemned already because he hath believed in the name of the only begotten Son of God (Jesus Christ)" (John 3:18 KJV).

Reverend Dr. John Thomas Wylie

Chapter One

Three Stages Of Salvation

In MOVING TOWARD THIS subject, it will assist us with keeping as a top priority that salvation is a act, a process, and a consummation. We may put the matter being referred to a question. Is a Christian saved, would he say he is being saved, or would he say he is to be saved later on? It is made plentifully unmistakable in the New Testament that he is each of the three-saved, being saved, and going to be saved.

It isn't our aim here to talk about finally these three phases of the topic. However, we do set out obviously that these three stages are to be found in the New Testament. The majority of what we need to state from here on will bear on one of these three parts of the topic.

We take up now an examination of the use of the verb "to save" and the noun "salvation" with a specific end goal to demonstrate that salvation is exhibited in these three different ways in the New Testament and in our experience. The utilization of these words (to save and salvation) isn't the only evidence. There are other terms used in the New Testament that confirm the matter.

Truth be told, the whole introduction of the Christian life clarifies that each of the three of these stages are central in the Christian experience. We will examine quickly these terms (to save, salvation) with a glance at some other facts, to show that salvation is regarded in these three ways in the New Testament.

Salvation As A Definite Act Or Transaction

In any case, these signify a clear act or transaction. It is this transaction that starts the Christian life. It makes one a Christian. In Luke 7:50 Jesus said to the sinful woman: "Thy faith hath saved thee." The verb here in Greek is in the perfect tense. This shows the saving was in some sense a transaction completed.

Obviously it alludes to the forgiving of the woman's sins discussed in verse 47. In Luke 19:9 NIV Jesus says concerning Zaccheus: "To-day salvation came to thy house." The verb here is in the aorist tense, which shows that salvation came to Zaacheus as a clear event.

In Ephesians 2:8 KJV Paul says: "By grace have ye been saved through faith." This is an perfect tense once more, signifying a transaction completed. In some sense the Christian has been saved.

In keeping in touch with Titus, Paul said in 3:5 that as indicated by his mercy, God saved us through the washing of regeneration. Here the apostle utilizes the aorist to denote salvation as a distinct act. (Cf. additionally Luke 8:12; John 5:34; 10:9; I Cor. 1:21, et al.)

Other than these uses of the terms to save and salvation, there are many others that talk about the Christian as having been forgiven, justified, reconciled, adopted, sanctified, et cetera. There is rich proof in the New Testament that the Christian life begins in a definite transaction and that this transaction is an act of salvation on God's part.

We are altogether as per the New Testament in thought and language if we speak of the Christians as one who was saved at a definite time in the past or as one who has been saved at some past time.

Salvation: A Process

We ought not be as per the New Testament, if we thought of God's saving action in the Christian's life as having been ended with this initial transaction. Not only does the Christian life begin in a clear act of salvation on God's part, but he additionally sustains and continues with this saving activity. The Christian life must be sustained.

It must be sustained by God's mercy. The redeemed life is not a self-sustained and self-contained entity. This act of God in saving the sinner conveys him into a new relation to God. Yet, the delinquent, in the wake of encountering the grace of God, can no more keep himself in a saved state than he could bring himself into such a state at first.

There is no stage of that life and no phase of it that is self-sustaining. Paul speaks in Romans 5:2 ASV about Christ as the One through whom we have access by faith into this grace in which we stand. If one should be disposed to underline the way that we stand in this grace, and that it is consequently our work, it would be with a specific end goal to notice that it is in the grace of God that we stand, the same grace by which we were justified; and that this faith is directed to the same Lord and Savior in whom we were justified.

Consequently, we see that the redeemed life of the Christian is definitely not an self-contained or self-sustained life; it is sustained by faith in the grace of the same Savior and Lord in whom we were justified.

In Ephesians 2:8 ASV Paul says that by faith ye have been saved – a perfect passive form of the verb. The perfect tense in Greek means something done in the past, however the force or effect of which proceeds to the present. So when Paul says that by grace ye have been saved, he implies that ye were saved in the past and continues to the present. And the continuation is as much God's work as the beginning was.

But, the Christian life needs not exclusively to be sustained; it needs to grow and increase. If it does as such, it must be by the grace of the same God who saved us at the beginning of the Christian life. There are a couple of places in the New Testament where salvation is talked about in this progressive sense.

In I Corinthians 1:18 KJV Paul says that to the individuals who are perishing the word of the cross is foolishness, but to those who are being saved it is the power of God. Here the words "perishing" and "being saved" are available latent participles and appear to be utilized in a progressive sense.

Those who are perishing are so blinded spiritually that they don't see anything but foolishness in the word of the cross, but those in the process of being saved experience in this word of the cross God's power for their salvation. We have a comparative utilization of both these expressions in II Corinthians 2:15 ASV. The messenger says that we are a sweet savor of Christ unto God, in them that are being saved, and in them that are perishing. Here, as in I Corinthians 1:18 KJV, he is by all accounts he seems to be speaking of perishing and salvation in the progressive sense.

These terms (to save and salvation) are rarely utilized, however, in the New Testament in an unmistakably progressive sense.

There is plentiful other evidence, nonetheless, that the Christian life is intended to be ordinarily a life of growth. The journalists of the New Testament continually utilized growing things to illustrate that life. Paul and the author of Hebrews showed awesome concern that their spiritual children should show progress in the Christian life.

They were upset when this was not the situation, as the third chapter of I Corinthians and Hebrews 5:11 ff. will show. In the passages from Paul, he reprimands, rebukes the Corinthians since they are still carnal and babes in Christ. The writer of Hebrews reproves his readers since they are still babes when they should be teachers. They should be full-grown (perfect) men.

Protestant theology has normally utilized the term sanctification to denote the development of the new life begotten in regeneration. The word seems to be utilized in that sense in places, however that is not really its characteristic use in the New Testament. (See for this use of the term Rom. 6:19,22; II Cor.7:1; I Thess. 4:3-4, 7, 13; I Tim. 2:13; Heb. 10:14; 12:14; I Pet. 1:2). Once more, a portion of these may be questioned, but hardly all of them.

Salvation: A Consummation

A third thing is still more unequivocally underscored in the New Testament than the way that the Christian life is normally a growing life;

to be specific, that the Christian is moving toward a glorious consummation in which his salvation will be completed.

In the Synoptic Gospels, Jesus shows that the kingdom of God is a present experience (Mark 1:15; Matt. 10:7; 10:9,11 et al), a growing reality (Mark 4:26-29, 30-32; Matt. 13:33), and something that is coming to a consummation (Matt. 13:30, 49-50; 25:31, et al.). In John's Gospel eternal life is mainly a present reality (3:36; 5:24; 6:47); but here likewise we find that there is a consummation to be expected (6:39-40, 44). God will raise up his people at the last day.

Paul lays extraordinary weight or stress on what the scholars (theologians) call eschatological salvation. He says that our salvation is closer than when we believed. The present resembles a dark night, but he encourages them to lift up their heads and look for the day (Rom. 13:11-14 KJV).

In I Corinthians 15, he dwells on the Christian's hope of the resurrection, which will consummate his salvation. Death is the last foe which Christ will conquer. In Romans 8:24 he says that we are saved by hope. The Christian looks forward with eager expectation to the day of final deliverance (Rom. 8:23).

Indeed, the whole creation, which has been subjected to vanity by virtue of man's sin, longs to share in this glorious consummation that is coming to the offspring of God (Rom. 8:19 ff.). Man's assurance that he will be at last delivered from transgression (sin) lies in the indwelling Spirit of God. This indwelling Spirit is the firstfruits of the coming harvest (Rom. 8:23 KJV).

The Spirit constitutes God's promise money, the earnest of our inheritance, God's pledge that he will complete the transaction begun in regeneration (II Cor. 1:22; Eph. 1:14). The Spirit is God's seal ensuring our final deliverance (II Cor. 1:22; Eph. 1:13; 4:30).

In I Peter 1:5, we have an instructive statement on the eschatological phase of salvation. Peter says that we are kept by the power of God through faith unto a salvation ready to be uncovered (revealed) in the last time.

Peter has just said that God begat us again to a living hope by the resurrection of Jesus Christ from the dead. He doesn't consider either end of our salvation as dissociated from the other. Neither Jesus, Peter, Paul, nor any other New Testament author thought of salvation as completed here. It begins here, but is completed in the future. It goes to its full completion "in the last time."

Salvation must be eschatological to be complete. It must be brought to finality. What Gods has begun he will complete unto the day of Jesus Christ (Phil. 1:6). This is the reason our salvation is by hope (Rom. 8:24). God has done much for the believer. But, what he has done is only the beginning. We look for better things. What he has done is the ground and basis of hope for what he will do; and what he will do is to grow out of and continue what he has done.

It will be the consummation of what he has done and is doing for us here.

This is in accordance with the faith that he is a God of purpose and of grace. He doesn't do something for us and then quit. What he does for us at any specific time is a part of his bigger plan for us. We don't see nor comprehend the complete plan. We don't realize what we shall be when he shall have completed his work in us. In any case, we realize that, when he shall appear, we shall be like him (I John 3:2 KJV). Furthermore, that is sufficient.

Chapter Two

The Nature Of Salvation

IN THIS CHAPTER WE don't propose to talk about in detail what happens in salvation. What we do wish to do here is fairly to inquire into the general nature of salvation. Prior to taking up a more itemized discourse of God's saving activity, we wish look into the nature of salvation, and also the phases of it just talked about. It will be seen that these two things-the stages and the nature of salvation-are firmly related and interlinked.

With regards to the general importance of salvation, three things may be called attention to:

It Is Deliverance From Sin

The word translated to save has for its general importance the idea of deliverance. It was utilized for deliverance from any kind of threat, danger or peril.

In the Old Testament the sign of God's favor was found in deliverance from sickness, disease, death, bondage, and a wide range of transient malice (temporal evil). This view was limited more to this life and to the visible and temporal world. In the New Testament the emphasis is changed. The main concern is with the spiritual and eternal world. We don't mean by this that New Testament Christianity is an "other worldly" religion. It concerns itself with this life and with the temporal world. But it is concerned about the temporal world for the sake of the everlasting.

The center of New Testament Christianity is in the coming of the eternal into time in the person of Jesus Christ. This does not reduce the significance of the temporal. It uplifts its significance. In any case, the seen and temporal world gets its significance from its relation to the spiritual and eternal. This world is certainly not a self-contained system. It gets its meaning in relation to a world that transcends above the visible and temporal.

So in the New Testament salvation is principally salvation from sin. We find that note in the Old Testament, particularly in a portion of the psalms and the prophets. In any case, it doesn't stand out in a clear and definite way that it does in the New Testament. Deliverance from fleeting shades of evil and deliverance from death have a considerably bigger proportionate emphasis.

But in the New Testament the huge thing that emerges is God's grace that saves from sin. In the Old Testament Moses and Joshua were national saints since they delivered Israel from her national adversaries and oppressors. yet, Jesus came to deliver from transgression (sin).

This may be thought of as the negative aspect of salvation, since it talks about deliverance from something. This would hardly be an exact thought, nonetheless, on the grounds that it is a positive something, just negative in form.

Salvation from sin can happen only by the incoming of a more greater power to claim man and displace sin in his life. A stronger one than the householder must come in if the householder is to be overcomed. Paul graphically sets this out in the seventh chapter of Romans.

The rule of the Spirit of life in Christ must displace the rule of sin and death (Rom. 8:2). In the event that one looks at an awesome backwoods of trees in pre-spring, secured with dead leaves, he require not make a fuss over how the trees will free themselves of the dead leaves. The coming to new existence with the entry of spring will make the dead leaves shed and offer place to crisp foliage. so man is delivered from the old existence of sin and wickedness by the inflowing of a new life in Christ.

Salvation Is A Development Of A Christlike Personality

If we would give an explanation that would be all-extensive regarding what salvation implies, we maybe couldn't improve the situation than to state that it intends to be made Christlike in character. This is our fate as the author of First John gives it. We don't know what we shall be, but we do know that, when he will be manifested, we shall be like him (I John 3:2).

This is God's purpose for us and the thing toward which he would coordinate every one of the components that come into our lives (Rom. 8:28-29 RSV). Jesus sets before his disciples as the goal of their endeavoring that they ought to be like God, which is to be like Christ (Matt. 5:48). This would incorporate being freed from sin. To be like Christ is to reject sin from the life.

One favorable position that Christianity has over other systems, from a moral (ethical) perspective, is Christianity has its ethical perfect set out as a concrete historical person.

If anybody wants to know what Christianity proposes to improve the situation man, he can discover by taking a look at Jesus. He is the embodiment of what God proposes to make men.

When unbelievers would reprimand Christianity as a present-day drive on the planet, that feedback typically appears as saying that the pronounced followers of Christ are not like him. That is typically viewed as the most lethal feedback that can be coordinated against Christianity in our present-day world. That feedback at any rate pays Jesus the compliment of yielding that he is the most astounding perfect that the critic knows.

In his teaching Jesus gives his ideal as to what a citizen of the kingdom of God ought to be. It is toward this perfect the Christian should move by the grace of God. It is also discernible that, when Jesus reveals to us what kind of a man a citizen of his kingdom ought to be, he is giving us a picture of himself. The picture of Jesus as given in the Gospels and the kind of man that he says the resident of the kingdom ought to be coordinate each other.

To be saved intends to be headed straight toward turning into that kind of a man. To be saved intends to enter the kingdom and to develop toward a perfect resident of the kingdom.

A correlation of Mark 9:43 and 45 with 9:47 will show that going into life and going into the kingdom mean the same thing. Mark 10:23,24, and 25 with 10:26 will show that entering the kingdom and being saved mean the same thing. To be saved one needs to enter the kingdom and to grow toward the ideal set by Jesus for kingdom citizenship.

It is noteworthy that in places in the Gospels the verb normally interpreted "to save" in the American Standard Version is deciphered "to make whole." In Matthew 9:21 KJV the woman with the issue of blood said that she could however touch his piece of clothing she would be made whole (truly, "saved"). Jesus said the woman thou was made whole by faith. In Mark 5:23 KJV Jairus implores Jesus that he (Jesus) will lay his hands on the daughter of Jairus that she might be made whole.

To interpret the word in these occasions "to make whole" is anything but a strict interpretation, however it is a genuine one. To recuperate a man physically or mentally was to make him whole. To recover one from sin is to make him whole spiritually.

To make one whole is to make him like Jesus. As somebody has genuinely stated: "Jesus was the only complete man the world has ever observed; the remainder of us are only fragments." To save us is to save us from being fragments into being whole.

Saved Man Will Have A New Habitation

A third thing to be considered as to the nature of salvation is that man renewed in the image of God will have a new environment.

This is what Paul alludes to as the heavenly kingdom (II Tim. 4:18 RSV). God's renewed people will occupy the new heavens and the new earth. This is the what people mean by heaven. It is envisioned in the book of Revelation as the New Jerusalem descending out of heaven to man. Jesus indicates that he is going to prepare a place for his people (John 14:2 KJV).

With many people the idea of place is essential in thinking about man's destiny. This is obviously a mixed up thought. The primary concern about any man isn't the place he is but what he is. Obviously, place or condition is critical, however it isn't so vital as character. Good environment don't make man glad and satisfied.

A terrible man conveys his own particular wretchedness inside himself. "My-self am hellfire." In one of his expositions Emerson suggests that one reason a few people are dependably in a hurry is that they are trying to get away from the hopelessness of a terrible self. In any case, Emerson additionally demonstrates that such a man can't discover surcease from his hopelessness since his wretchedness is simply the aftereffect of his terrible, and a man can't get away from an awful self by setting off to somewhere else. When he arrives, that same bad self will be there and the wretchedness that definitely inheres in it.

Then again, there is where it counts in the human heart the conviction that the good man should be glad and that the terrible man does not have the right to be, and won't be cheerful. Thus, it will turn out to be at last. So, as well as at last man's external home will relate to his internal condition and character.

This isn't in every case valid in this life. In some cases the good have the slightest of "common luxuries" and common flourishing, and the devilish succeed and develop fat. This is perceived in both the Old and New Testament. In any case, it is additionally perceived in both this ought not be valid, and won't be forever.

In a few places it turns into an unequivocal issue to the faith of the holy people. The essayist of a portion of the psalms demonstrates that he is puzzled by such a confusing circumstance. It is managed finally in the book of Job. The disciples confront the issue in John, chapter nine, when they meet the man conceived blind.

In the story of the rich man and Lazarus, Jesus demonstrates that the upright may suffer here however will be blessed in the next life, while the wicked who prosper here will be punished after death (Luke 16:19 ff.).

A standout amongst the most educational entries in this issue is the thing that Paul gives in Romans, chapter eight. Paul shows that the Spirit of God stays in the Christian. This comprises one a Christian and gives one an awareness of the fact (Rom. 8:9, 12 ff.). The Spirit makes the Christian long for complete deliverance and look to the time when he shall realize his glorious destiny (Rom. 8:23 KJV).

Not only does the Christian yearn for deliverance, but the whole creation also longs to partake in the glorious destiny that awaits the children of God (Rom. 8:18 ff). No doubt, Paul expected a glorious environment for the glorified holy people. A few people attempt to disclose to us rather unquestionably about where and what this condition is to be, yet the Scriptures hardly appear to justify such a position.

Chapter Three

Union With Christ

To THIS POINT WE have considered something of the nature and stages of salvation. For what remains, we wish to consider more definitely the initiation of the Christian Life. When God saves the sinner (initially), just what does he do for him? What takes place when one becomes a Christian?

Our salvation is in Jesus Christ. By this is meant, not only that our salvation comes from Jesus Christ, but also that it is due to the fact that we are brought into a vital relationship to him.

Set Forth In The New Testament

This reality set forward in many ways in New Testament. Particularly is it taught in John's Gospel, in the First Epistle of John, and in the compositions of Paul. These compositions are mystical as in they set forth continually and certainly this essential relation of the saved with Christ.

In John's Gospel, Jesus is the light of the world (9:5); he is the bread of life (6:35); by eating his flesh and drinking his blood we abide in him and he in us (6:56); he is the great shepherd in whose hands we security (10:27-28); he is the vine, we are the branches (15:1 ff.); he is in us, we are in him (14:20).

Paul likewise utilizes various articulations that put forward this union with Christ. Jesus Christ is the head, we are the members of his body (Rom. 12:4 ff; I Cor. 12:12 ff.); he is the husband, the church is the wife (Eph. 5:22 ff); he is to us what the foundation is to a building (I Cor. 3:10 ff; Eph. 2:20). We are crucified with Jesus Christ (Gal. 2:20); we are risen with him (Col. 3:1); we are buried with him in baptism (Rom. 6:4); we suffer with him and we will be glorified with him (Rom. 8:17).

In union with him, Paul says he can do all things (Phil. 4:13). Particularly in Ephesians and Colossians Paul always talks about being in Christ and of Christ being in us. In one place he goes so far as to state: "To me to live is Christ" (Phil. 1:21). By this he appears to imply that for Paul to live in the world means that Christ lives again in and through Paul.

Faith The Means Of Union
With Jesus Christ

The means by which union with Christ is established and maintained is faith. In John 6:56, Jesus says that we eat his flesh and drink his blood, we live in him and he in us. The parable of the vine in John 15 demonstrates that to abide in the Lord and carry on with a life of faith means the same thing.

In John 6 when Jesus talks about eating his flesh and drinking his blood, he is discussing the act and attitude of the soul in which we appropriate Christ as our life and salvation. In Galatians 2:20 RSV, Paul says that the life which he now lives, which is Christ living in him, is by faith in the Son of God.

In Ephesians 3:17 KJV Paul appeals to God for the Ephesians that Christ may abide in their hearts by faith.

It is a question as to whether this life in union with Christ ought to be discussed as mystical. Some would call this Christian mysticism. Others protest considering mysticism anything that is Christian. They do this on the ground that mysticism is non-rational-a matter of losing oneself in God or the All in an unconscious or super-conscious state. If mysticism is to be related to such an unconscious state or super-conscious rapture, this union with Christ ought not be called mysticism.

Paul and others may have had conditions of rapture of which they could give no balanced record. (See II Cor. 12:1 ff.). However, it would be a mix-up to recognize the life in Christ with such encounters. Paul himself appears to respect them, alongside talking in tongues (I Cor. 14), as superfluities and extravagances of the Christian life instead of being of its essence. However, being joined to Christ by faith isn't a luxury or superfluity. It is of the essence of that life. It is that without which the Christian life can't be.

This life is mystical as in sense that a Power outside of and beyond man lays hold of him, comes into his life and takes possession of him. It is super-rational in the sense that it is beyond man's power thoroughly to comprehend. But, so are numerous unavoidable truths or facts that apply to life-one may state, every one of the unavoidable truths that apply to life.

The fact that this life in Christ is by faith is a guarantee that it won't be a life of blind unconscious or super-conscious mysticism. The gospel of Christ is a gospel of truth. No one in the New Testament underscores this more than Paul.

Paul contends, argues, urges, induces, works day and night that his believers (converts) might be intelligent. He doesn't think about a believer as one who blindly stumbles into the Christian life. He thinks rather about the Christian as one who hears and apprehends in a intelligent way the truth as it is in Jesus Christ, at that grows in the Christian life by constantly growing apprehension and appropriation of that truth.

With these writers (Paul and John), as everywhere else in the New Testament, faith is an intelligent act. It is as a matter of first importance perception and appropriation of the truth. The life in union with Christ is a life of faith, and faith without the component of wise intelligent apprehension would not be faith.

Union With The Living Christ

The conception of union with Christ by faith has no meaning apart from the New Testament teaching that Jesus is presently the risen, reigning Lord. "The faith that that looks back to the historic Jesus; it looks up to the living Christ. Christ is a living person with whom we must be vitally joined by faith if he saves us from our transgressions (sins).

The cry "back to Christ," which means back to the historical Jesus of the Synoptic Gospels and far from the transcendent Christ of Paul and John, is a motto that means to devitalize Christianity, for merely a historic Christ can't save. He must be super-historic. Indeed, the Christ of the Synoptic Gospels is just as transcendent as the Christ of John and Paul. However, some of the critics think they get in the Synoptic Gospels a Christ with no element in him that can't be measured as far as human life and history.

The Christ who is presented in the New Testament as the object of saving faith is the Jesus who having been slain by wicked hands was raised from the dead by God (Acts 2:23-24; 5:30-31). He is the Christ who in the Spirit can be called Lord (I Cor. 12:3). We don't merely reach back by a stretch of imagination over nineteen centuries to the Jesus of history; we reach up by faith to the Christ who lives and rules at the right hand of God.

The Christ with whom we were united by faith isn't only the person who rose from the dead and lives forevermore; he is the Eternal One. He is One who said of himself: "Before Abraham was born, I am" (John 8:58). The fact that he was eternal made it possible for Abraham to see his day.

Abraham saw him as One who transcends time. He is the one in whom all things consist and unto whom all things were created (Col. 1:16-17 KJV).

He is the One who is the effulgence of God's glory, the very image or reproduction of his substance, and who upholds all things by the word of his power (Heb. 1:3 KJV).

Union With God

This union with the living Christ is union with God. The hugeness of this union with Christ is that in him we come to know God with everything that suggests. To discuss union with Christ means nothing if he is nothing more than a historic character whom we know through the New Testament records.

These records are essential, for the Christ we know in Christian experience isn't another than the historic Christ, yet he is more than historic. He not only carried on with an existence in time and space, but in his resurrection and ascension he transcended the historic order. Furthermore, when we know him as the transcendent Christ we are conscious that in knowing him we know God.

Our consciousness of union with Christ and with God are indivisible. No man knows the Father aside from the one whom the Son wills to reveal him (Matt. 11:27 KJV). For a knowledge of God we are totally subject to and dependent on Jesus Christ his only begotten Son. However, in an inquiry between knowing God in Christ and knowing God outside of Christ. It is a choice between knowing God in Christ and not knowing him at all.

The claims of Jesus in this regard are completely consistent with experience and have been vindicated in experience. Outside of an experiential knowledge of Jesus Christ as Savior and Lord, men may guess about God and come to hold certain suppositions about him that are right; however they never come to know God himself. But, by faith in Jesus as Savior and Lord men

Dr. John Thomas Wylie

are vitally united to God in an experience that establishes such a knowledge of God as means to nothing less than salvation from transgression (sin).

The Gospel of John which puts such a great amount of stress on union with Christ also reveals to us that to know Christ is to know God. This Gospel reveals to us that there is no other way to know him. No man has seen God at any time; the only begotten Son who is in the bosom of the Father he has declared him (1:18). Furthermore, Jesus Christ stated: "He that hath seen me hath seen the Father" (14:9 KJV).

Union With Christ Through The Spirit

This union with Christ is something that happens in the realm of spiritual experience. We have said that the Christ we know in this experience is more than the Christ of history. He isn't another Christ, yet he is more than the Christ of history. What's more, our knowledge pf him is of a higher order than that in which we know the facts of history or of regular day to day existence.

Paul says that no man can call Jesus Lord save in the Holy Spirit (I Cor. 12:3 KJV). The Christ we therefore know is time-transcending in nature. He is eternal and spiritually omnipresent. He goes with his people to the last place and to the consummation of the age (Acts 1:8; Matt. 28:20).

This Christ can't be known apart from the Spirit of God, and knowing him is a recreative experience. It gives a different tone and quality to one's whole experience and life.

Paul says that if any man is in Christ there is new creation (II Cor. 5:17 KJV). It is a transaction in which God's creative power through his Spirit is at work in the realm of character and producing a new result.

This union with Christ isn't to be translated after the pantheistic design. Our union with Christ does not mean the losing of the limited (finite) self in the endless All (infinite). The surrender of our wills to the will of God in Christ does not mean the losing of our wills. It doesn't intend to cancel personality. It doesn't mean the throwing off of moral responsibility by merging oneself in the impersonal Absolute. It means rather the finding of oneself. The prodigal son went home to his father when he started thinking clearly (came to himself) (Luke 15:17).

One never comes to himself until he comes to Christ. When one comes to Christ he discovers his will fortified, his mind quickened, his moral nature renewed-he finds himself.

Chapter Four

God's Saving Act

EACH BLESSING THAT WE enjoy as Christians grows out of our union with Christ. A full discourse, thusly, of union with Christ would include everything that follows as to salvation. So we will take up next what God does for us in Christ.

In this we see that by faith we are carried into union with Christ. Accordingly we are carried into a new relationship with God. God does something for us. The most general term used in religious philosophy (theology), and maybe in the New Testament, for what God does for us is salvation. In any case, there are many routes in the New Testament to speak to what God does for us in Christ. Some of these we will now consider.

In Christ God Forgives Our Sins

When man sins against God two things result. Man is separated from God, and God's displeasure comes on man. In saving us man's separation is changed in his repentance and God's disappointment or displeasure is removed.

Sacred texts putting forward the thought

As officially expressed, in Old Testament times emphasis was laid on different types of deliverance, for example, deliverance from adversaries (Psalm 27:1 ff; Jer. 23:5 ff.), deliverance from illness (Psalm 49:14-15 KJV). However, even in the Old Testament salvation from sin was the chief blessing. We may take look at a few several passages in which forgiveness of sins is set forth.

In Psalms 32 David discusses the blessedness of the man "whose transgression is forgiven, whose sin is covered." The Lord does not impute to him iniquity, and in his spirit there is no guile. So long as he kept quietness (silence) and refused to confess his sin, God's hand was heavy upon him; he was scorched with the drought of summer. But when he confessed his sin, the Lord forgave the iniquity of his sin. We have a close parallel to this in Psalm 51.

This psalm is even yet a work of art, and will be to the end of time, in which a soul convicted of sin pours out its confession to a God of mercy and pleads for forgiveness and cleansing. The penitent in each of these cases has come to perceive that sin has broken his fellowship with God and that there is no possibility of peace and joy for him until his transgression (sin) is forgiven and he is cleansed from its defilement.

In Psalm 103 RSV, alongside the blessing of being healed of illness, praise is attributed to Jehovah since he forgives sin (v. 3). He doesn't deal with us after our sins, nor reward us as according to our iniquities (v. 10). As a result of his transcendent lovingkindness (v. 11) and fatherly pity (v. 13), he removes our transgressions (sins) as far from us as the east is from the west (v. 12).

In Jeremiah 31:31-35, the prophet tells about a new agreement (covenant) that Jehovah will make with his people. This covenant will not resemble the old covenant that he made with them in delivering them from Egypt. That covenant they didn't keep.

This covenant will be founded on a more prominent (greater) deliverance than the deliverance from Egypt. It will be founded on a deliverance from transgression (sin). He will forgive their evildoing (sin), and their sin will he remember no more. This will give such an inner knowledge of God that they will keep this covenant. By this forgiveness the knowledge of God will be placed in their hearts.

In the New Testament the forgiveness of sins is one of the key blessings that men were to receive in the messianic salvation. John the Baptist was to "go before the face of the Lord to make ready his ways; to give knowledge of salvation in the remission of sins" (Luke 1:76-77 KJV).

Forgiving of sins was one of the essential blessings that Jesus taught his disciples to pray to God for (Matt. 6:12; Luke 11:4). After the resurrection Jesus commissioned his followers to preach, in his name, remission of sins, upon the condition of repentance, to all the nations (Luke 24:47 KJV).

Peter declared to the people at Pentecost that after repentance they should be baptized unto the remission of sins (Acts 2:38 KJV). He preached to Cornelius and the company gathered at his house that the prophets all bear witness that through the name of Jesus each one who believes on him receive remission of sins (Acts 10:43).

In Ephesians 1:7 ASV Paul says: "In whom (Christ) we have our redemption through his blood, the forgiveness of our trespasses" (cf. Col. 1:14). This appears to distinguish redemption and forgiveness of sins; at least, it makes forgiving the central element in redemption. Without forgiving there is no redemption.

This rundown of passages is by no means exhaustive, but it is illustrative of the teaching of the Bible regarding the matter. It shows that forgiveness of sins was the essential blessing of the good news of Christ.

That thought was not obscure to Old Testament holy people, but rather the thought turns out in its clearness and fulness in the new dispensation.

The book of Hebrews shows that the forgiveness of sins was a fundamental element in the new covenant. It was in the forgiveness of sins that men should know God (8:11-12). This was in accordance with the prophecy of Jeremiah (Jer. 31:31-34 KJV).

The Meaning Of Forgiveness

We may ask somewhat more especially with respect to what is implied by the forgiveness of sins. The term translated "to forgive" in the New Testament means to send away. It is precisely our term to remit, send back or away. To remit sins is to put them away. Yet at the same time the inquiry stays: To secure in what sense? What does it mean to put away sins?

It doesn't intend to secure in any mechanical or spatial sense. Sins can't be put away thus. To remit sins is clearly an interesting expression, a figure of speech. Here and there the issue was thought of as practically equivalent to the discharging of an indebted person. Jesus thought of it in this way when he encouraged the disciples to pray: "Forgive our debts as we forgive our debtors" (Matt. 6:12 RSV).

We have the great proclamations in the Old Testament that God puts our transgressions (sins) behind his back (Isa. 38:17) and recalls them no more (Jer. 31:34). He throws them in the profundities of the sea (Micah 7:19). He washes us, and makes us whiter than snow (Psalm 51:7).

It isn't precisely consistent with say that to forgive sin is to make us as though we had not sinned. This isn't valid in the awareness of the sinner. The awareness of an forgiven sinner isn't the same as the consciousness of one who has not sinned. "Once a sinner always a sinner-in this sense at any rate, that he who has however once trespassed can never be as though he had never trespassed. His very blessedness to eternity is an different thing from the blessedness of the sinless. The man whose evildoing isn't ascribed is an altogether different being from the man whose wrongdoing (sin) was never committed.

Forgiveness does not imply that sin is removed as an obstruction to our fellowship with God. Sin breaks man's fellowship with God. It is a personal offense against God. "Against thee, thee just have I sinned, and done what is evil in thy sight" (Psalm 51:4 RSV). "Your iniquities have separated between you and your God, and your sins have hid his face from you, so that he will not hear" (Isa. 59:2 RSV).

As the Holy One of Israel, Jehovah won't accept the offerings of a wicked, sinful and rebellious people, nor hear their prayers. They must repent of their transgressions (sins) and do the right (Isa. 1). But when sin is forgiven, the block to fellowship is removed. The cloud that close out the face of God is rubbed out. In this sense sin is remitted, sent away.

It resembles the revival of human fellowship after companions or friends and family have been isolated by a wrong done by to each other. Forgiveness looked for and obtained the previous closeness of confidence, intimacy and love. It is this that provides for one the inspiring feeling of freedom, peace, and joy after realizing that his sins are forgiven. He is released from the subjugating feeling of blame, guilt. An incredible weight (burden) is gone from the soul.

A new light comes in. Often the whole face of nature is by all accounts seems to be transformed. A joy unspeakable and brimming with glory comes into the soul. We understand that we are loosed from our sins (Rev. 1:5), which have bound and oppressed (enslaved) us.

Forgiveness is a personal act that law, physical, social, or good, can't explain. Law remains unaware of forgiveness. There are those today who demand that law reigns on the planet, and that there can be no variety from the rule of law; law is incomparable, perpetual, and that law is supreme.

It doesn't have any effect what shape the law may take; it might be physical law or it might be moral; law speaks the last word, forgiving is prohibited. There can be forgiveness only where personality and personal relations are the ultimate reality.

God is a person and God is more than law, physical or moral. If a man does not have faith in a personal God, he can not have faith in forgiving of sins. Then again, the experience of the forgiving of sins gives one such an assurance of relationship with a personal God that one can not lose the consciousness of God without likewise losing the sense of forgiven sin.

This transcendent act of God is a act that not only delivers with it the possibility of God's personality; it is likewise an act of grace on his part. All things considered it transcends law. Grace does not invalidate law, but rather it transcends law. Law can not forgive, but God can. Law can not forgive, since law knows nothing about grace. Grace is a personal quality. It is the most elevated possible nature of good quality, moral character.

Law can not have character. Character has a place only with a person or in other words, only a person has character, not law. Forgiving, thusly, is an act of grace on the part of a personal God; and in this act the God of grace transcends but does not violate or nullify law.

While this transcendent personal act on the part of God removes sin as that which blocks our fellowship with him, it doesn't immediately remove all of the consequences of our transgressions (sin). It doesn't remove us from the physical, chronicled, social, and order of things with which we are associated. It does show man's superiority to this order. It reveals man as of more worth than the whole order of things to which he belongs and of which he is the climax and goal.

It demonstrate that man is not enslaved in that order. It demonstrates that this order exists for man. Man is the master of the order of things. Nothing demonstrates the transcendent worth of man and his mastery of the world order like the grace of God that forgives sins.

The grace of God that forgives sins and restores the sinner to the fellowship of a heavenly God will at last deliver the forgiven sinner from all the insidious consequences of his sins. This is genuine both with reference to the individual and to the redeemed race.

Sin broke man's fellowship with God and brought spiritual death, trailed by a swarm of shades of malice, evil consequence upon sin and spiritual death. When sin is forgiven, man's fellowship with God is restored and as a consequence every one of the ills that followed upon transgression will be removed, but this can not be done at a bound. To do as such would likely mean fiercely, violently to dislocate man from his historical, social, and moral connections as a member from the race and as a part of the order of nature.

For example, a body that is maimed by sickness or disease, caused by transgression, is not more often than not, or at least restored to perfect soundness upon the forgiveness of sin. If one squanders the quality of youth in extravagant living (riotous living), God will happily forgive the humble reckless when he returns home, but the substance of his physical and sometimes his psychological masculinity (mental manhood) isn't given back to him in this life.

Once more, the social aftereffects of our transgressions (sins) are not always at once counteracted when our sins are forgiven. God forgave David his horrendous sins regarding

Bath-sheba and Uriah, yet the sword never withdrew from David's home until his passing.

Many a severe tear he shed over the consequences of his sins, in spite of the fact that he knew the sweetness of God's forgiving grace. We see this unmistakably in the matter of physical death. The heart of the punishment of sin is spiritual death. In any case, the physical death came as a result of sin. When one is forgiven, spiritual death is removed and the sinner is restored to fellowship with God.

This implies at last in the end death in its completeness and totality will be removed, however not this side of the resurrection. There are implications, likewise, that the whole natural order will be renewed in the final consummation of things.

In any case, while we are not without a moment's delay delivered from all of the consequences of our sins, when we are forgiven, we are placed in such a relation with God, to the point that every one of the ills of life may end up redemptive powers in our lives working for the one purpose of transforming us into the image of Christ (Rom. 8:28 ff.).

The experience of the forgiveness of sins as a gracious act on God's part, not only removes sin as an obstruction to fellowship with God, yet in addition gives one a insight into the character of God that generally would be incomprehensible, impossible.

As such, the forgiven sinner understands God, and therefore has a fellowship with God, that would be inconceivable for a man who had never trespassed. How could a man who had never trespassed comprehend the component in God's character that we express by the term grace?

The grace of God is the most glorious element in his character as indicated by the Christian view. This grace we know only in its redeeming work in our lives. An immaculate being can never know a God of grace. The conception would have no significance to him. Now and again the evangelist says that God may have sent blessed messengers (angels) to report the gospel to sinful men rather than of sending redeemed sinners. Be that as it may, without a doubt of it, this is doubtful. What might an unfallen blessed messenger (angel) think about grace of God that saves a sinner?

The sinner who has experienced God's redeeming grace knows, and can make the other sinner know, something of that grace. He has a knowledge and an insight, and undying love for a God of grace that an unfallen sinner, man or heavenly angel, will be a stranger to forever.

Redemption in Christ, then, does not return man in the place of an unfallen Adam. It puts him on a new basis, gives him an insight into God's character and fellowship with God that such an Adam would never have. It, along these lines, gives him a kind of holiness that would be unimaginable for such an unfallen man.

For example, the redeemed sinner will, because of an ordeal of God's grace in saving him, have imitated in his life the spirit of grace in relation to his colleagues. This is found in that the redeemed man has in him the spirit of grace as showed in his evangelistic and missionary spirit. Such a spirit isn't something incidental or accidental in the Christian life; it is of the essence of Christianity.

An unfallen Adam may take care of business of legalistic justice; he could hardly be a man of grace. Henceforth the redeemed sinner will be a better man than the unfallen Adam would ever have been. This does not intend to pardon or to overlook sin but rather to glorify the grace of God.

We may state, the forgiveness of transgression (sin) is the essential blessing in salvation, and that the forgiveness of sins through the grace of God changes the whole of life into a redemptive order. The ills of life that before were of a very basic level retributive angle currently turn out to be fundamentally remedial and redemptive in that they can, by God's grace, be made to contribute to the development of Christian character.

Chapter Five

Objections To The Doctrine Of Forgiveness

WE MAY NOW THINK about two objections to the doctrine of forgiveness of sins through the grace of God. One is a protest to the doctrine from the stance of the divine nature; the other is with reference to the assumed impact of the doctrine upon the life of the forgiven sinner.

The primary objection is that the doctrine of forgiving isn't consistent with the unchangeableness of the divine nature. God can't change, we are told. So the change isn't in God, it is in the sinner. It resembles riding a bike against the breeze. While one is riding against the breeze, he feels the power of the breeze opposing him and keeping him down.

However, when he pivots and rides with the breeze, he feels the breeze bearing him on. Thus, while living in transgression and opposing God, one is aware of the heavenly obstruction; yet when one straightens out himself in his relation to sin and God, he feels the perfect love and approval bearing him on toward the goal. In any case, similarly as it was not the breeze but rather the rider that changed, so we are advised, it isn't God that changes, but man.

At the point when man changes, he feels as though God had changed. This is at times carried to the extent of denying that God changes in his attitude toward the sinner. All the change, we are told, is in the sinner.

Be that as it may, while the facts confirm that the sinner changes when he repents of his transgression (sin) toward God, this just states one side of the issue. God does not change in his attitude concerning the individual or the race, in his characteristics or his temperament, yet God changes in his attitude toward the sinner when the sinner changes. God isn't the slave of his own unchanging nature. Nor is God an impersonal power. He is a moral personality. As a person he can will. As moral his attitude isn't the same toward the sinner and the righteous.

This objection would not just make forgiveness incomprehensible; it would make any fresh start on God's part impossible. There could be no miracle. The incarnation is logically ruled out on this ground. God couldn't have willed at a clear point in history to enter into an essentially new relation to the race in the person of Jesus Christ.

Creation also would be incomprehensible. So would recreation or regeneration. Revelation as an act of self-disclosure on God's part goes, as well; on this view revelation is only man's feeling after, and maybe his revelation of some truth about God. Everything unmistakable in Christianity would vanish on this view. God turns out to be just an impersonal force and his immutability turns into the stagnation of death.

This objection falls in with the view that denies that God pronounces upon the sinner any judgment. As guilt is deciphered to mean just a guilt consciousness, so forgiveness is translated to mean only a subjective feeling on the sinner's part, not including any change on God's part. The change was in the sinner.

In any case, we should demand that forgiveness is more than a subjective feeling to which corresponds no objective reality. We must keep up this position that we would do justice either to the biblical teaching or to Christian experience. Forgiveness is God's act. He changes his attitude toward the sinner. It is the apprehension of this changed attitude on God's part that conveys peace and joy to the sinner's heart.

This is essentially indistinguishable objection from the one considered a couple of paragraphs back in which forgiveness was denied on the ground of the inviolability of law. It makes no difference whether God is enslaved by his own changelessness (immutability) or the invariability of law; in either case his personal activity in forgiving sin is denied, and in either case salvation in the Christian sense of the term is impossible.

The perspective of forgiveness implied into this objection answers to the perspective of sin that speaks to the guilt consciousness of the sinner but denies or ignores guilt consciousness of the sinner's relation to God. In the event that there is no objective guilt, there is no need of an objective forgiveness. If God does not condemn sin, there is no need that he should forgive. If on the other hand, God as a holy God condemns sin, the only hope for the sinner is in God's forgiving grace. If sin, as committed against God's holiness, breaks man's fellowship with God, then the only thing that can renew that fellowship with God, at that point the main thing that can restore that partnership is to have the guilt of sin removed in an act of remission that puts away the guilt of sin.

The other objection to the doctrine of forgiveness as an act of grace on God's part is that it will urge the sinner to live in sin. Will God's benevolent forgiving of sin urge the forgiven sinner to live in sin? We reply, No; however then again it will deliver from sin.

Quickly think about a few explanations behind this answer. Initially, on the grounds that forgiving is based on the redeeming work of Jesus. Sin isn't forgiven without a adequate expression of God's heavenly displeasure against sin. In the cross of Christ God condemned the world's transgression (sin).

Let nobody imagine that forgiveness is a nice thing, either for God or for man. If one imagines that forgiving is a simple issue, let him recollect how hard it is for man to forgive his individual man; for society to forgive the individuals who abuse its traditions and decencies; for the state to forgive the criminal. Forgiveness costs God much. It cost him his best, even his only begotten Son. It is in the blood of Jesus that we have redemption, even the forgiveness of our trespasses (sin) (Eph.

1:7; Col. 1:14). It is in the blood of Jesus that we are loosed from our sin (Rev. 1:5).

Also, on the grounds that our forgiveness is conditioned upon our repentance. In repentance we repudiate sin. We condemn sin with something of the same hatred and awfulness of it that God had for it in condemning it in Christ's cross. This is a progressive, a regenerative experience. One can never think, feel, or act toward sin as he did before repenting.

This is brought out in what Jesus says in regards to our forgiving as being conditioned on our forgiving our fellow man. Jesus says that we forgive not, neither will the Heavenly Father forgive us (Matt. 6:15). How demanding of unimportant, vindictive human instinct!

Forgiveness is such a revolutionary experience, that one can't claim it except if he finds imitated in his own attitude toward his fellow man something of God's gracious attitude toward him. Only as God's grace reproduces itself in us can we be able to claim that grace has nullified sin in us. Except if our fellowship with the God of grace is real that find ourselves in an exceptionally practical and searching way manifesting a genuine communion of that grace, we can't claim that our sins are put away by his grace.

"There is forgiveness with thee that thou mayest be feared" (Psalm 130:4 RSV).

What a feeling of reverence, of awe, of holy horror for sin and righteous fear of God did we find in our hearts when first we found that by faith in the crucified One our sins had been remitted; and with every passing day the wonder grows, our horror of sin deepens, and our reverence fear of God, the God of all grace, increases.

We see, that forgiveness is not just the remission of penalty. If that is all that forgiveness implied, it would not be salvation from sin; it would only cancel the evil outcomes of sin and leave man in sin. What men need to see, what they will see if they truly repent, is that the colossal evil isn't punishment for sin, but sin itself. When God forgives, sin itself is undone. At the end of the day, it is a transaction that changes a sinner into a saint, a holy person.

In Christ We Are Justified

Justification in the New Testament is a Pauline teaching (doctrine). No other New Testament author utilizes the term to any obvious degree to express salvation. In one of his illustrations, Jesus talked about the publican as going down to his home advocated as opposed to the Pharisee (Luke 18:14). For Paul this is the principle term for communicating what God does for the believing sinner.

The Doctrine Defined

Notice that it is something that God does for the sinner. There is such a mind-bending concept as the justification of the righteous. This implies that the righteous is vindicated as being righteous and on the ground that he is righteous. It is in this sense the word is utilized when it is said that the wisdom is justified of her children (Luke 7:35); that is, the children of wisdom act so as to vindicate the ways of wisdom.

Once more, Jesus reveals to us that the publicans and every one of the people "justified God," on hearing the message of John the Baptist, by responding to the message and following up on it, while the Pharisees and legal advisors rejected for themselves the advice of God (Luke 7:29).

The people justified God by responding so as to state that God was right. They embraced, endorsed God's message as given by his messenger. Paul joins the significance of Psalm 51:4 KJV, "that thou mightest be justified when thou speakest," in Romans 3:4 KJV when he says, "That thou (God) mightest be justified in thy words," thus showing God to be in the right.

We have no trouble in understanding this utilization of the term. It implies that one who apparently is in the right is endorsed as being so. The upright man or cause is vindicated as being righteous. The trouble comes when we are informed that God justifies the ungodly(Rom. 4:5).

Paul's doctrine is that the sinner, who has been under God's judgment (condemnation) by virtue of his sin, upon condition of faith in Christ, is forgiven and received into God's favor. The trouble lies in the way that the teaching is incomprehensible (paradoxical). Paul states and defends the doctrine of justification by faith at length in his epistles to the Galatians and to the Romans.

In these epistles Paul sets out this doctrine of justification by faith over against the idea of justification by works. He affirms that the last is impossible. No flesh shall be justified in God's sight by works of law (Rom. 3:20). That kind of justification would be a justification of the righteous. It would basically be an acknowledgment of man's goodness.

All things considered, God would just give man acknowledgment for what he had earned; he would pay him what was his (man's) expected due. Whatever God did for man would be in payment of a debt (Rom. 4:4).

The paradox of Paul's doctrine is that God does not justify the righteous but rather justifies the sinner. He justifies the unrighteous rather than the righteous. God's justifying act here is something in excess of an acknowledgment of man's accomplishment; it is more than a declaration of the status quo.

In Paul's doctrine he stresses that justification is by grace on God's side and by faith on man's. It isn't something that man accomplishes; it is something that man receives. Man gets what God gives. Paul emphasizes that it is a blessing, a gift on God's side, a gift of grace.

The theme of the book of Romans is found in the expression "the righteousness of God." Paul utilizes this expression in two senses. He utilizes it to assign a quality in God's character. It indicates a characteristic of the Divine Being. It is utilized in the sense in Romans 3:25-26 when the witness informs us concerning work of Christ as showing the righteousness of God.

Here the author obviously implies that God's character is appeared to be righteous and so as to demonstrate that he is a righteous God thus that his character isn't compromised in saving us.

However, Paul utilizes this expression, the righteousness of way that he saves sinners in Christ. God deal with us in an different sense, even in this same paragraph. In Romans 3:21-22 KJV, he speaks of "the righteousness of God" as something that God bestows on men in Christ upon condition of faith. He has finished up an argument to demonstrate that all men are sinners and that nobody can be justified by works of law.

Justification or righteousness is something that God gives, not something that man gains.

In Romans 1:17 KJV, Paul says that in the gospel "is uncovered a righteous nature of God from faith unto faith." He constructs this with respect to an Old Testament message: "The righteous shall live by faith" (Hab. 2:4). He along these lines associates this righteousness of faith received as a blessing, a gift from God with the Old Testament. He says that this righteousness of God revealed in the gospel is witnessed by the law and the prophets (Rom. 3:21 KJV).

In referring to David (Psalm 32) and Abraham (Gen. 15:6) as cases of justification by faith, along these lines making the principle of justification by faith the unifying principle of the Old and New Testaments.

In summing up the significance of this doctrine, we may underscore three things:

One is that it is justification of the sinful. God must justify the righteous if men are to be made a decision based on their own achievements. Be that as it may, there are none righteous before God. All have sinned and fall short of the glory of God (Rom. 3:23 ASV).

Jew and Gentile-all men-rest under the judgment of God. men could be justified by the deeds of the law in the event that they could keep the law; but no man does this. The disappointment isn't in the law, yet in the weakness of the flesh (Rom. 7:12; 8:3 KJV).

The justification of the sinner implies that, when the sinner has faith in Christ, he is delivered from the condemnation resting on him on account of his sin, and is received into God's favor. He is accepted of God by virtue of his faith in Christ rather than condemned on account of his sin.

The second thing is that men are justified on the condition of faith. Faith is set over against works of law. We don't acquire our accepted with God by deeds of law; we receive it as God's free gift. It is by faith on our part, since it is by grace on God's part (Rom. 4:16). God gives, we receive. Our faith appropriates what God offers in mercy.

Now and then the contention is made that, since our salvation is conditioned on faith, then after all it depends upon something that we do. Then it is said that it could rely upon baptism or some other recommended condition as well as on faith. This misconstrues the idea of faith.

Faith can't be placed in the classification of works that man does. Paul set it over against works of law by way of contrast. Justification by faith is the antithesis of justification by works. Justification by works is an arrangement by which man tries to put God under commitment to him by playing out specific things required by God. Justification by faith is an arrangement, a plan in which man gives up all claim on God, recognizing that he can do nothing to justify God's blessing.

Rather than claiming something from God, he gets something as a gracious blessing, a gift. Faith then isn't a work. It is the sinner's acknowledgment that he can do nothing and that whatever is done for him must be done by a God of mercy. Faith gives up all effort to do for oneself and gives way for God to do. It isn't accomplishing something, it is getting self off the beaten path (getting self out of the way) so God can so something.

The third thing is that Justification by faith is based on Christ's work for us. The faith that justifies isn't a reliance on something that the sinner does for himself; it looks rather to Christ and what he has done for us. Justification by faith is grounded in work by Christ on our behalf. It is through the redemption that is in Jesus Christ that we are justified (Rom. 3:24). We are justified in his blood (Rom. 5:9).

Summary Of The Values Of The Doctrine

We may sum the issue up, by saying the doctrine of justification by faith has the following qualities in the religious life:

1. It gives one confirmation of acceptance once for all with a holy God. This it does on

the grounds that it perceives that the sinner's acceptance with God is on the ground of Christ's redemptive work. The sinner puts his trust in Christ and his redemptive work for acceptance with God.

Since Christ's offering was complete, made once for all, the sinner has assurance of a permanent, once-for-all acceptance with a God of righteousness.

2. Since it gives this affirmation of acceptance with God based on the redeeming work of Christ, it brings spiritual peace, joy, and freedom (Rom. 5:1 ff.). It is, consequently, the only teaching that can meet legalism. It gives freedom from the law strategy for salvation and sets the spirit free to serve God in love and joy.

Christ puts an end to the law method of obtaining righteousness to everyone that believeth (Rom. 10:4). That is, Christ puts a conclusion to the law technique for getting righteousness and brings in the strategy for faith. Along these lines subjugated dread is supplanted by dutiful trust. The old Jewish strategy for endeavoring to gain righteousness with God is invalidated, made bankrupt, by Jesus Christ, and, along these lines, the bondage of the letter is supplanted by the freedom of the spirit. If the Son will make you free, ye will be free for sure.

3. The doctrine of justification by faith is the only premise whereupon which righteous people can be developed. Insofar as men endeavor to procure salvation, their lives will be servile and self-centered. Be that as it may, faith in Jesus Christ with reference to our acceptance with God takes us up our selfishness and faces us out to serve God and men.

Chapter Six

In Christ We Are Reconciled To God

THIS IS ANOTHER TERM utilized by Paul to indicate God's act of saving the sinner. This term implies basically the same as justification. It sees sin as causing a alienation or estrangement between God and man. At the point when this alienation is removed the sinner is said to be reconciled to God.

That reconciliation is synonymous with justification is found in Romans 5:9-10. In verse 9 Paul discusses being justified in the blood of Jesus; in verse 10 he speaks of being reconciled to God through the death of his Son. Plainly these two articulations allude to a similar experience. Paul's statement in II Corinthians 5:19 shows the same thing, for he characterizes reconciliation as being the non-imputation of trespasses.

An inquiry emerges with respect to reconciliation is whether man's reconciliation to God comprises in the expulsion (removal) of man's enmity toward God, or whether it is the removal of God's displeasure toward man, or whether it is both. It has been contended that since the reconciliation is always discussed as man's reconciliation to God and never as God's reconciliation to man, it implies the removal of man's enmity toward God and not the removal of God's displeasure toward man.

Be that as it may, the two passages just alluded to as demonstrating that reconciliation and justification are synonymous would demonstrate that this translation of the issue isn't right. If reconciliation is synonymous with justification, the non-imputation of transgression (sin), it involves a adjustment in God's attitude toward man.

A same thing can be shown in another way. In Romans 5:10 Paul talks about our being reconciled to God as foes (enemies). What is implied by our being foes? In the event that we can discover the response to that inquiry, it will assist us with answering the inquiry concerning what happens when we are reconciled to God.

Does Paul mean by our being foes to God that we are at enmity with God, or does he mean that God condemns us? Fortunately we have another utilization of this term in the same letter that will answer that inquiry. It is in 11:28. Talking about Israel he says: "As touching the gospel, they are enemies for your sake; however as a touching gospel, they are beloved for the fathers' sake."

Here their being foes is set over against their being beloved. Furthermore, since their being beloved plainly depicts God's attitude toward Israel, the former term couldn't be restricted to Israel's attitude toward God. In Romans 5:10, when Paul talks about the enemies of God being reconciled, he doesn't mean by enemies merely those who have enmity toward God, but he implies these enemies who are reconciled of God implies the removal of God's displeasure as well as the removal of man's enmity toward God.

There is an statement from Jesus that demonstrates the same thing. It is found in Matthew 5:23-24. Jesus says that if one brings his gift to the altar, and there recalls that his brother has ought against him, he will leave his gift before the altar, go and be reconciled to his brother. Note that his brother has something against him, yet Jesus says he is to be reconciled to his brother.

For him to be reconciled to his brother means to remove his brother's enmity, not simply to dismiss his own. So for the sinner will to be reconciled to his brother means to remove his brother's enmity, not simply to dismiss his own. So for the sinner to be reconciled to God means that the sinner shall receive the pardoning grace of God. Doubtless it is meant to describe a mutual transaction, but the emphasis seems to be on the removal of God's displeasure in the non-imputation of sin.

In Christ We Are Adopted Into The Family Of God

The term adoption is by all accounts used in three detects, or rather with reference to three distinct applications. In Romans 9:4 Paul utilizes it with reference to Israel as a country in her relation to Jehovah. In Romans 8:23 he utilized it with reference to the redemption of he body in the resurrection for which the Christian tensely is standing by. However, the typical utilization of the term is with reference to our being made God's children spiritually when we become Christians.

The term is a legal term, as justification seems to be, and means the demonstration by which one not normally a child is made lawfully the child and beneficiary of the person who adopts him. The term, be that as it may, isn't to be taken as portraying just a legalistic exchange. Paul in Romans 8:15 and Galatians 4:5 underscores the conscious ownership of the Spirit regarding our adoption or as an outcome of it, and demonstrates that by this conscious ownership (possession) of the Spirit we are delivered from the bondage of fear and legalism.

He also calls attention to the way that as an outcome of our adoption, we not only are made children of God bet in addition heirs, and, along these lines, inherit with Christ all the spiritual riches of God.

It is clear that this term is, on one side, synonymous with justification, and on the other, with regeneration. It is a lawful term like justification used to portray what God does for us in saving us. Justification stresses the removal of the condemnation of sin; adoption emphasis our new standing as sons in relation to God.

Like regeneration, it puts our salvation in terms of sonship-adoption being the lawful term, regeneration the experimental or biological term. The two thoughts are so closely related that we won't dwell on adoption here but will pass on to discuss regeneration.

In Christ We Have New Life

Some New Testament terms utilized for this thought.

A standout amongst the most well-known terms in theology and in preaching depict God's saving acts is the term regeneration. Our term new birth means practically the same. The term regeneration has gone into religious phrasing for the most part from the influence of the expression of Jesus in John 3:3,7, where he talks about being begotten or born again or all the more proper from above.

Peter utilizes the same word (compounded with a preposition word) in I Peter 1:3,23. There are other terms in the New Testament used to portray this experience of being renewed in the grace of God. One is Paul's figure of a new creation. In II Corinthians 5:17 KJV, he says: "If any man is in Christ, he is a new creature" (truly, "there is a new creation"). Here the messenger depicts this saving act on God's part just like an creative act in which he so renews one that "the old things are passed away; behold, they are become new."

He says in Galatians 6:15 KJV: "For nor is circumcision anything, nor uncircumcision, but a new creature" (literally, creation). In Ephesians 2:10, 15; 4:24, and in Colossians 3:10, he utilizes a same figure. In Romans 2:29 Paul says that true circumcision is that of the heart, in the spirit, not in the letter. This obviously alludes to regeneration as that which makes one a member of the true spiritual Israel.

Another figure found in Paul's compositions and in some other places is that of death and resurrection. In Romans 6:1 ff., Paul put forward the idea that the Christian is one who has died to sin and ascended to walk in the newness of life. This dying to sin may be put forward in test terms as meaning repentance. To die to sin is to repent in the event that we take a look at it as a human act; if we look at it from the perspective of the divine efficiency, it is identical to regeneration.

In Galatians 2:20 KJV Paul says: "I have been crucified with Christ; and it is no longer I that live, but Christ liveth in me." In Galatians 6:14, he glories in the cross through which the world has been crucified to him and he to the world. (See likewise Gal. 5:24 and Col. 2:20.) This helps us to remember the expression of Jesus that if any man would come after him, he must deny himself and take up his cross.

One will lose his life by saving it and save it by losing it (Matt. 16:24-26). "But a grain of wheat fall into the earth and die, it abideth alone; but if it die it beareth much fruit" (John 12:24 KJV). "The hour cometh, and now is, when the dead shall hear the voice of the Son of God; and they that hear shall live" (John 5:25 KJV).

The Need Of Regeneration

The need of regeneration has been shown in general in our discussion of the doctrine of sin. In studying the doctrine of sin, we saw that sin was all inclusive (universal) and that man was defenseless in its power. In this sense man is completely corrupted (depraved). He is altogether helpless in the power of sin except if and until delivered by the grace of God.

In we take a look at the moral (ethical) and religious standard set up for men by Jesus, we see without a moment's delay the need for regenereation. His standard was a high expectation or standard. If men get into the kingdom of paradise (heaven), they should have a righteousness surpassing that of the scribes and Pharisees (Matt. 5:20). The righteousness of the scribes and Pharisees was external and legalistic. Jesus demanded a righteousness that was internal-a righteousness of thought process, purity of heart and of outward life (Matt. 5:21 ff.).

The regenerating grace of God is the only thing that can give men the graces of character requested in the Sermon on the Mount of the those who are to be subjects of his kingdom. Jesus said that we should be perfect as the Father in heaven is perfect (Matt. 5:48).

He recognized the law as demanding love for God with all of the powers of one's being and love for one's neighbor as one loves himself (Luke 10:25 ff.).

Such a standard brings only despair unless one is given some spiritual powerful dynamic other than is to be found in the normal man.

The need regeneration turns out unmistakably in Paul's discussion of the power of sin in human life. This is appeared in the 6th and seventh chapters of Romans, particularly the seventh, in which he gives his very own chapter out of his own spiritual experience. He portrays his condition of unconsciousness of condemnation (v. 9a), his awakening to a knowledge of the demands of the law and his sense of condemnation and death that followed (vv. 9b-11), his endeavors to break the power of sin (vv. 15 ff.), lastly his miserable sob for help (v. 24).

Then comes his triumphant victory in Jesus Christ (v. 25). In the eighth chapter he says that the law (rule or dominion) of the Spirit of life in Christ Jesus liberated (freed him) him from the law (rule or dominion) of sin and death (v. 2). This thing that the law couldn't do has now been done; sin has been condemned in the flesh; that is, its power has been broken by the incoming of a power superior to the power of transgression (sin), to be specific, the power of a new life in Jesus Christ (v. 3).

Nothing short of this new life in Jesus Christ would do. The old man couldn't be developed into submission to the will of God, "for they that are after the flesh mind the things of the flesh" (v. 5). "The mind of the flesh is death" (v. 6) "The mind of the flesh is enmity will against God: for it isn't liable to the law of God, neither to be sure would it be able to be; and they that are in the flesh can't please God" (vv. 7-8).

Some have thought that Paul's statements here are unduly dark, critical and pessimistic. They have charged it to his Pharisaism and have tried to forget this dark picture, the sinfulness and helplessness of the natural man as not belonging to Paul's best Christian thought. In any case, this record demonstrates that this doctrine isn't just the remaining parts of Paul's Pharisaic dogmatism but grew up out of his own experience under the law and under grace.

When he states how the carnal mind is set against God and can bring only condemnation and death, he is just telling us what he knows from his own experience.

The Nature Of The Change

What sort of a change is regeneration? Would could it be that happens when a man is born again? 0

1. Some may state that there is no use to talk about that inquiry, for the change is a mysterious one and subsequently, can't be comprehended. Things being what they are, it might be stated, what is the use to try to comprehend it?

Would regeneration be able to be comprehended? Actually no, not by any stretch of the imagination. It is a riddle, yet so is most everything else we manage. Jesus revealed to Nicodemus that it resembled the wind-as much as to state that the blowing of the wind was as much a puzzle as regeneration; yet we realize that it blows. So it is with the commonest actualities and encounters of life.

Matter is baffling, personality is strange, will is puzzling, love is mysterious. However we know something about these. Yet, we don't have the foggiest idea about any of them. Regeneration is a reality of experience, and we know something about it as a reality of experience, similarly as we probably am aware any of alternate substances said.

In trying to comprehend what sort of a change regeneration is, there are two wellsprings of data open to us, every one of which is basic to the end in see. One is the New Testament educating with respect to the issue; the other is encounter our own and that of others whose declaration is accessible for us.

We have seen that the New Testament uses an assortment of articulations to depict this transaction-most or every one of them analogies drawn from different domains of life and encounters to attempt to set forward the idea of this transaction. The plain reality that such huge numbers of various terms are utilized is prove that we are managing an ordeal whose central criticalness it is hard to set forward.

However by an investigation of these, particularly in the light of our own encounters of the regenerating power of God's grace, we can know something of the nature and hugeness of this experience.

Surely one would be advocated in accepting both of two states of mind concerning the issue. One is to state that, since it is mysterious, there is no use to attempt to discover anything about it.

That would be proportional to stating that, since we can't thoroughly understand it, there is no use to endeavor to discover anything about it. To assert that it is mysterious is to say that we know something in regards to it. To realize that there are points of confinement to what we know merits something

The other mentality we ought not expect is the state of mind of dismissing or rejecting the thought since we can't completely comprehend it. If we will acknowledge just that which we see completely, what amount of will we acknowledge? Our statement of faith would be brief undoubtedly on that sort of a premise. We would not have faith in our own reality, for that is obviously an extremely baffling thing. However we acknowledge the reality whether we can comprehend the depths of its significance or not.

The change is principally of the nature of a moral and spiritual renewing. It is a change the principle importance of which is to be found in the domain of character. In this change the fundamental moral disposition is changed. The affections and exercises of life never again focus on self, but in God.

Love for God and for one's colleagues turns into the controlling element throughout everyday life. One dies to sin and ascends to walk in the newness of life (Rom. 6:1 ff.). It is troublesome for some to keep from thinking of regeneration as the addition of some kind of substance, or some new faculty to one's being.

The "new creation," (II Cor. 5:17 RSV), the "new life" that never perishes (John 5:21), the "divine nature" of which we are partakers (II Peter 1:4),-these, they think, must mean the addition of a new metaphysical element or component or substance to one's being, and not a "mere" change in moral disposition.

Dr. Strong (2014) appears to be nearly to think about the issue along these lines, when he discusses our sharing in a new humanity, of which Christ is head. In any case, let it be said that there is nothing that could happen to any man of more basic and broad importance than a change in moral disposition.

This is truly a new creation. It is of such colossal hugeness that Paul can state in view of it that old things are passed away; they are become new (II Cor. 5:17 RSV).

A true philosophy is coming to see that the central idea with respect to the reality isn't "substance," however personality. The most important thing about personality is the ethical nature of the individual, the question of character. A specific sort of non-evangelical theology has taken its slogan as of recent years "Salvation by character," which means by this the advancement of character inside and of oneself as opposed to reliance on the "merits" or "imputed righteousness" of another.

This "new religious philosophy or theology" is right in its emphasis on the possibility that there can be no salvation apart from character. There can be no salvation for man other than really making him righteous. And to the degree that an uneven conventional Protestantism has discussed being saved by an "imputed righteousness" aside from any righteousness of our own, as if we didn't need to be made righteous, he could go to paradise on a righteousness transferred to our credit by a mere trick of bookkeeping-to the degree that it has meant that or established the connection that it implied that, to that degree has it merited the disdain of all personalities of any moral observation or reality.

A justification that implied close to that would for sure give one is to make him equitable, and one isn't spared aside from as, and to the degree that, he is made honorable. Be that as it may, there can be no bona fide and perpetual righteousness apart from the grace of God showed in Jesus Christ.

The grace of God embodied and made accessible for us in Jesus Christ is the reality of central noteworthiness for us. Insofar as one neglects to discover and proper God savingly uncovered in Christ, he misses the way for righteousness and truth. Presently regeneration is a transaction in which the ethical or moral nature is changed so that one can never again rest in an life of sin.

Righteousness turns into the passion of the soul. This does not imply that all underhanded or evil affinities are at a stroke disposed of from one's being; however it means that such a revolutionary transaction has occurred in the soul that it can never rest until it is free from transgression (sin). The overwhelming passion of the soul progresses becomes love for righteous and hatred for sin. In principle the soul is made sinless.

This is the reason the man that is begotten of God can't sin. He can't live in wrongdoing (sin) as his normal and native element as some time ago he did; he can't constantly sin, can't consistently sin; he can't carry on with a life of transgression (sin) (I John 3:6-9 KJV).

This change is one that is wrought in the moral nature of man by the Spirit of God. Only divine power could create the change. Both experience and Scripture bear testimony to this. It is a new creation in which old things pass away and all things are made new (II Cor. 5:17 RSV). It is a birth from above in which one is cleansed (born of water) and given a spiritual disposition(born of the Spirit) (John 3:3ff.).

It is a change that isn't of blood (natural descent), nor of the will of man (human nature on its higher, spiritual side), but of God (John 1:12 KJV). God's power works this change. The gospel is the power of God unto salvation (Rom. 1:16 KJV). God attracts men to Christ (John 6:44 KJV). The Spirit convicts of transgression (sin) (John 16:8-11). This was manifested on the day of Pentecost. It was after the Spirit came that men hearing the gospel were pricked in their hearts and cried out, saying, "What shall we do?" (Acts 2:37 KJV).

All through the Acts and Epistles we find that it was the Lord who wrought with the disciples to save. No man can call Jesus Lord except in the Holy Spirit (I Cor.12:3). Paul may plant and Apollos water, however God must give the increase (I Cor. 3:6). It is unto God that salvation is ascribed in the book of Revelation (12:10, et al.).

Christian experience takes the stand concerning a same truth. The man who experiences regeneration knows as well as he knows sunlight from murkiness that he himself did not work the change. He submitted to God, and God transformed (changed) him. He knows the power that deals with him as something new in his experience. He knows it as some power different and higher in nature than the social powers that influence his life. It is the spiritual motivation of the Christian heart to express gratitude toward God for one's own salvation or for the salvation of another.

The Divine Spirit regenerates us by reproducing in us the moral and spiritual image of Jesus Christ. The thing that God had at the top of the priority list for us in pre-destinating us to salvation is that we will be made like Jesus Christ (Rom. 8:29). It is in Christ that we were chosen before the foundation of the world (Eph. 1:4).

We don't know yet what our eternal destiny is to be, yet we do realize that, when Christ shall appear, we shall be like him, for we shall see him as he is (I John 3:2 RSV). In regeneration one is crucified with Christ. The old man dies and Christ comes to live in us. By faith we are united to him that he becomes the inner motive power and dominant passion of our lives. (See Gal. 2:20 RSV).

This was so true for Paul that he could state of himself, "To me to live is Christ" (Phil. 1:21

KJV). We are in some cases enticed, tempted to think about the saving work of the Spirit as being detached and unrelated to the person and work of Christ. This is an error. The Spirit came to bear witness to Christ (John 15:26; Acts 5:32). He regenerates us by making Christ to dwell in us the hope of glory (Col. 1:27).

This demonstrates, while the Spirit regenerates us, commonly in any event the Spirit utilizes means in renewing us. It is by the word of God that we are begotten again (I Peter 1:23 KJV). Maybe it would be going too far to state that God couldn't regenerate a man without the use of ordinary gospel agencies; yet we positively are safe in saying this is his typical way.

We need not be dogmatic in limiting God to the utilization of such means. We can allow the infinite One some freedom to work in manners that we don't comprehend or know about. However when that is stated, maybe we are still justified in saying that God regenerates, at any rate as a distinct experience, such as brings one into conscious fellowship with God, only by using gospel agencies that gives one a knowledge of Jesus as Saviour. This is necessary in light of the fact that man is a rational being.

He isn't saved in some enchanted or magical way that has no relation to his rational and moral nature, but by coming into conscious fellowship with Christ. This is the purpose of what one may call Paul's philosophy of missions in Romans 10:12 ff.

This carries with it the idea that man is regenerated by faith. Through faith are we sons of God (Gal. 3:26 KJV). To as many as received him gave he the right to become the children of God (John 1:12 KJV). Faith is a regenerative act, since it carries one into union with God as revealed in Christ.

There has been an age-long discussion among Calvinism and Arminianism concerning which goes before, faith or regeneration. Calvinism has said that regeneration as God's quickening act must be first, on the grounds that a dead man can't act. An unholy man can't perform a holy act. At that point, it is stated, to hold that man exercises faith before being quickened into life would hold that man inside and of himself accomplishes something that brings the favor of God, and that can't be permitted.

Then again, the individuals who hold the other position say that, if one is regenerated before he exercises faith, at that point man is saved without his own consent and God deals with him as a thing and not as a person.

We are once in a while informed that we are not to consider both of these as coming in front of the other in purpose of time, but that one goes before the other logically. The Calvinist says that sensibly regeneration must go before, since God's power is the cause for man's act; so God's quickening action causes man's response in a demonstration of faith.

The Arminian, in any case, says that confidence coherently goes before, since faith is the condition of salvation. It is scarcely conceivable that each is correct. Taken a look at in another way, faith may sensibly go before; took a look at in another, the quickening power of God may go before. A more accurate way for communicating it is to state that faith and regeneration imply one another; they are indivisible; they are two parts of one spiritual experience.

We should recall that we can't have one without the other. You couldn't have a believer who was unregenerate, nor a regenerated man who was not a believer. The Calvinist is right in demanding that the power of God must regenerate and that man can't within and of himself believe. God must deliver faith in his heart.

Then again, the facts demonstrate that men are regenerated by faith. By faith we become the children of God. God regenerates. In any case, he doesn't regenerate irrespective of man's faith. He regenerates by producing faith in man's heart. What's more, regeneration isn't complete until man exercises faith. In the act of faith on man's part regeneration is completed. So the inquiry with respect to which goes before, regeneration or faith, becomes a good for nothing, meaningless question.

Chapter Seven

In Christ We Are Sanctified

Meaning Of The Term

It is standard now in treatises on theology to talk about the precept of "sanctification." This term is utilized in the Bible in a twofold sense. That is to say, as a matter of first importance, sanctification or commitment to God. This utilization is frequent in the Old Testament and isn't unknown in the New Testament. Utilized in this sense it included things and people and did not have moral significance.

The Temple, the sacred place (altar), the city of Jerusalem-anything associated in a special way with Jehovah and his service were talked about as holy. We speak today of the Holy Land, the Holy City, holy days, et cetera. Yet, the words holy and holiness came to have moral essentialness in the Old Testament. So do the terms sanctify and sanctification in the New Testament.

Things are sanctified as they are consecrated to God, as they are viewed and regarded as consecrated or devoted to divine service. In any case, since the character of God was viewed as ethically righteous, it was perceived that men who are worthy (acceptable) for his service must be additionally righteous in character. This contemplation is given extraordinary emphasis in places in the Old Testament, particularly in the psalms and the prophets.

When applied to people in the New Testament, the thought is on a very moral)ethical). The thing that makes sanctification important is man's lack of righteousness or his transgression (sin). The term is utilized in the New Testament both for the initiation of the Christian life and for its development. The New Testament talks about all Christians as "saints" or "sanctified ones" (Acts 9:13; Rom. 1:7; I Cor. 1:2; II Cor. 1:1; Eph. 1:1; Phil. 1:1; Col. 1:2). In this sense the term is synonymous with justification or regeneration.

This is sometimes called positional sanctification, as recognized from progressive sanctification. Then it is utilized with reference to the progressive cleaning or purification of the soul (I Thess. 5:23; Heb. 12:14). It is in this sense the term is usually utilized in discussions in systems of theology. Be that as it may, there are very few places in the New Testament where the term is unquestionably utilized in the sense of a progressive work. The preponderating use of the term is in its application to a definite act at the beginning of the Christian life.

Each Christian, at that point, anyway flawed he might be is sanctified in the sense that he is committed or consecrated to God by the power of the Spirit and by his own act of faith. One element in faith is surrender to Christ as Lord. Faith is thus an act of devotion or dedication. One commits himself to God and isolates himself from everything that opposes his consecration to God.

There should to be-ordinarily there will be-a deepening consecration to God and his service, and a more complete separation of oneself from all forces and factors of life that hinder this consecration; but this is just the carrying out of what was associated with that first act of consecration.

Every Christian is sanctified also in the sense of an inner purification or change (transformation) of character. In this sense sanctification means about the same as regeneration. One who is dedicated or devoted to God of love and righteousness will essentially become like him in character.

The thing that renews one in heart and character is the way that he is dedicated by a act of self-surrender to a righteous God. Fellowship with a holy God produces holiness in man. Here again there should be progressive sanctification ; but the overall prevailing use of the term in the New Testament is in the sense of the initial dedication or cleansing from sin.

Every one of these terms that we have examined are diverse methods for portraying what God does for us at the beginning of the Christian life. What God does is spoken to as forgiving, as justification, as reconciliation, as adoption, as being born again, as sanctification. There were different terms utilized, however these are the main ones.

Being brought into fellowship with God in Christ is such an awesome and wonderful transaction, that the scholars of the New Testament have utilized a rich assortment of expressions to give us some conception of the glories of what it means. They have held it up before us and turned it all around like an awesome jewel blazing its excellence back to us from numerous angles.

We have lost a portion of the magnificence and extravagance of their description by reducing their expressions to rigidly technical terms and dealing with them as sensible abstractions. Every one of these terms are distinctive ways for speaking to what God does for a soul at the beginning of the Christian life, when that soul is brought by the power of God's grace out of a life of sin into fellowship with God in Christ.

Chapter Eight

The Conditions Of Salvation

WE WILL CONSIDER WHAT are normally called the conditions of salvation. By this we mean the spiritual attitude one must assume in receiving the grace of God that saves from sin. As such, what must one do to become a Christian?

There are numerous terms utilized in the New Testament to portray the experience of becoming a Christian. Maybe to the basic elements can all be summed up in the two terms repentance and faith. It is no mishap that the experience of becoming a Christian has two principal perspectives, for in this experience man is concerned about two essential relations of life.

One is his relation to sin; alternate, his relation to God as a God of grace, revealed in Christ as Savior. The internal abandoning of sin is repentance; turning to Christ as Savior is faith. Each infers the other. Neither is possible without the other.

At the same time and in the same act that one abandons sin he turns to Christ. Sin and Christ are the contrary shafts of the ethical (moral) universe and one can't abandon one without turning to the other.

Repentance and faith are not two acts or moral attitudes; they are two parts of one act or attitude.

Repentance

Other Terms Used To Describe Repentance

Repentance isn't the only term utilized in the New Testament to describe the act or attitude meant by that word. Jesus says: "If any man will come after me, let him deny himself, and take up his cross, and follow me" (Matt. 16:24). To deny oneself intends to disavow, renounce, self as corrupt, sinful and selfish; to renounce the old self as unworthy. To take up the cross is to die; to die to the old self and give oneself to a New Master, Jesus Christ.

Jesus says likewise: "Whosoever will save his life will lose it" (Matt. 16:25 KJV). To lose one's life here is to give it away to another, to offer it to Christ and one's colleagues in service. He put this over against saving one's life so as to lose it. To save it (in order to lose it) intends to keep it for one's self, to carry on with the self-centered life.

To lose it (in order to save it) is to renounce the self-centered life. Paul talks about Christians as those being crucified with Christ (Gal. 2:20), and about those who have crucified the flesh with the affections and the lusts thereof (Gal. 5:24). He glories in the cross through which the world has been crucified to him and he to the world (Gal. 6:14). All these are diverse ways for communicating the possibility of repentance.

What Is Repentance?

The term that is interpreted repentance in the New Testament implies a difference as a primary concern (a change of mind). This includes three things.

a. Either as an element in repentance or as a point of reference condition, it includes the comprehension of one's condition as a sinner. One must come to acknowledge something of the guilt and condemnation of his sin. This conventionally discussed as conviction of sin. A few scholars talk about it as the scholarly element in repentance. It comes because of hearing gospel truth and the enlightening work of the Holy Spirit.

One can't atone until he comes to see something of the nature of his sin. This does not imply that the conscience of sin must be available in the same shape and to a same degree for every situation.

Now and again the consciousness of sin may take form as a sense of guilt and condemnation. In others it might be the sense of moral disappointment. Be that as it may, for each situation the knowing about the gospel strengthens this consciousness of sin.

In some cases at first it is a vague uneasiness, a consciousness that some way or another things are wrong with us. The hearing of the gospel heightens and clears this, with the goal that becomes a definite consciousness of sin. Sin comes to be viewed as sin. This implies it comes to be viewed as against God. As found in relation to a God of holy love it comes to be seen in its actual true character.

b. A second thing involved in repentance is that the love for sin will die in one's heart. This is typically talked as the emotional element in repentance. One may see himself obviously as a sinner and even comprehend the ruin involved in sin, but unless the love of sin dies in the heart, it will make no difference in his life. He has not repented.

This isn't to be related to fear of punishment. One may have fear of punishment without gospel repentance. This fear of punishment may deliver what has been named "hell-scared religion." But unless there is something more in one's religion than the fear of punishment he will not escape punishment.

This fear of punishment might be strengthened into remorse of conscience, so that one has no rest day or night. Be that as it may, remorse of conscience isn't repentance. In other words, repentance is a gospel grace, not just a perspective produced by a knowledge of the law which brings a message of condemnation for sin, but no message of salvation from sin.

One may frequently have extraordinary emotion in light of sin yet then not repent. He may openly sob, yet when the emotion passes he returns to his old sins. The emotional element in true repentance may be portrayed as "godly sorrow that worketh repentance" (II Cor. 7:10

ASV). It is a sorrow that grows out of a genuine comprehension of our sin as it is related to a God of grace. It is contrition. "A broken and a contrite heart, O God, thou wilt not despise" (Psalm 51:17). When one has this contrition because of sin, it will lead on to the third and final element in repentance.

c. The third element is in the renunciation of sin. It is the denial of sin by an act of will. Since the love for transgression (sin) died in man's heart in one's heart, there is a repugnance of one's whole moral nature against it. Sin is denied, less in light of the fact that one sees sin in its actual nature and comes to despise it.

This prompts a changed life as to sin. "How can we that are dead to sin live any more drawn out in that?" (Rom. 6:2 ASV). A wonder such as this is an ethical or moral inconceivability. Repentance is never total until the point that the will thus repudiates sin. This repudiation of transgression and a contrite heart because of sin always go together. They are two parts of one state of mind.

This demonstrates the change of mind here talked about isn't just a scholarly change. The mind incorporates the whole moral nature of man. To decide isn't just an act of the mind. To repent is to think back over one's course, to see its unsoundness, the wrongness of it, and decide to change.

It is no superficial matter; it goes down to the depths of the moral life. This change is an inward change. It is such a change as revolutionizes one's life in relation to sin.

Repentance And Reformation

There might be a stamped change in the external life following repentance, or there may not be. Here and there detestable propensities have so secured themselves on to the existence that such an inward upset is the main thing that will change them. In some cases there might be a marked change in the propensities for life without such an inward transformation. All things considered you have reformation without repentance.

In some cases the outward life may have been so right, made a decision by the norms of social ethical quality, that no uncommon outward reformation was needed. So you have reformation without repentance, or you may have repentance where reformation is excluded.

We are not to close, notwithstanding, that since reformation isn't needed at times repentance isn't needed. Reformation as customarily discussed implies a change in which vicious moral habits are left off. A man may have no vicious moral habits, however yet need to repent of sin toward God. Not all men are terribly indecent, grossly immoral, but rather all men are sinners. Sin is against God. Repentance is a religious act or attitude (of mind) of sin against God. Repentance is the renouncement of sin against God.

Atonement, subsequently, is a religious demonstration or mentality of brain. It isn't just the renouncement of sin; it is simply the revocation as malicious and wicked. It is to deny oneself and take up the cross (Matt. 16:24 KJV). It implies death to the sinful self.

Chapter Nine

The Christian Life A Life Of Repentance

WE OUGHT NOT CONSIDER repentance as being a demonstration performed at the beginning of the Christian life, not needing be repeated. It is an attitude that belongs the Christian life as a whole. The underlying act of repentance is the beginning of a life of repentance. Jesus says we should take up the cross day by day (Luke 9:23 KJV). Paul says that Christians have died to sin (Rom. 6:2 KJV), however he likewise exhorts them to reckon themselves to be dead to sin (Rom. 6:11 KJV).

The sinful self must be crucified every day. The old man, as Paul calls him (Col. 3:9 KJV), has a bigger number of lives than the notorious feline. He won't remain dead when killed. As a rule the most deepest repentance does not come at the beginning of the Christian's life. When one initially rises up out of the darkness of sin, his eyes are not yet acclimated enough to the new light of the gospel to see sin in the entirety of its horror. The more one lives in fellowship with a holy God, the more one consider himself to be sinful and corrupt. It's anything but an indication of special piety to hear one boasting of his own goodness. The term good is one that Jesus says men should use with a good of caution (Mark 10:18 KJV).

Repentance And Conversion

It is some of the time said that conversion is the external change relating to repentance, or repentance and faith, as an inner change. In some cases it is said that conversion is comprised of repentance and faith-repentance and faith being the elements in conversion. Neither of these is objectionable. Conversion implies a turning. It is that change as is evident, or winds up evident, to men. In that sense, it is an outward change. However, when Jesus talks about conversion, he lays emphasis on the inner characteristics of mind and heart. He says that one must turn and become as a little child in order to get into the kingdom of God (See Matt. 18:3 KJV).

Faith

The Meaning Of Faith

Faith is the part of conversion in which the soul turns to Christ for salvation. As shown above, it is indistinguishably associated with repentance. Since repentance is a believing response to truth of the gospel concerning us as sinners, it may be included in faith. In a few places in the New Testament we discover faith alone expressed as the condition of salvation; in others we discover repentance alone; in still others we find both; while in others yet we find different terms conveying the same meaning as these terms.

Faith is a term of such rich content and deep significance that it is hard to characterize in a simple proclamation. Christian faith, may be defined as trust in Jesus Christ as Savior and surrender to him as Lord.

a. Christ the object of faith. This suggests faith is something more than belief of a doctrine or the acknowledgment of a doctrine. No doctrine, however imperative, can be the object of faith in the full sense of the term. One can trust a person with his keenness. He can confide in a man with his heart or will. Nor is the church the object of faith. The Roman Catholic Church makes faith understood surrender to the church, so one is promised to put stock in the domain of doctrine what the church prescribes to be accepted and hone in the domain of morals what the church recommends to be practiced.

One has faith in Christ only on the authority of the church. In any case, this misses the mark regarding Christian faith. It is without a doubt a deadly depravity of faith. It puts the church in imperative regards where Christ has a place and calls for submission to the church, for example, a Christian can yield only to Christ. It oppresses the mind and inner voice to the church and its hierarchy order.

The place of doctrine in relation to faith is to introduce Christ to us as the object of faith and afterward to help clarify the importance of Christ as we probably are aware of him in experience. Doctrine, at that point, has an imperative place in the life of faith, however no doctrine all things considered can be the object of faith.

Christ is the object of faith by virtue of the way that he is the incarnation of God and is, in this way, the disclosure of God's saving grace. He is the object of saving faith since he is the person who atones for sin and is thereby the person who achieves redemption for us.

Faith in Christ and faith in God are indistinguishable. We can state that we trust in Christ for salvation or that we trust in God through Christ. In the New Testament and in Christian experience, faith in Christ is faith in God.

Maybe the importance of faith can be made a little clearer if we help ourselves to remember two aspects of the act of saving faith.

One is that in saving faith we get Christ as Savior. There are numerous methods for communicating this in the New Testament. It is coming to Christ. "Him that cometh to me I will in no wise cast out" (John 6:37 KJV). "Come unto me, all ye that labor and are heavy laden: (Matt. 11:28) KJV. It is called receiving him. To many as received him, to them gave he authority (or power) to become the children of God (John 1:12 KJV).

It is called eating his flesh and drinking his blood. Christ says that except if we eat his flesh and drink his blood, we have no life in us; but, if, we eat his flesh and drink his blood, he abides in us and we in him (John 6:52-59 KJV).

This announcement of Jesus has no reference to sharing of the Lord's supper, however it refers to what our sharing of the supper symbolizes. In the Old Testament this act of faith is known as a looking. "Look unto me, and be ye saved, all the ends of the earth" (Isa. 45:22 KJV). It is known as a hearing. "Incline your ear, and come unto me; hear, and your soul shall live" (Isa. 55:3 KJV).

Men are said to call upon the Lord. "It shall come to pass, that whosoever shall come unto me; hear the name of the Lord will be saved (Acts 2:21; Rom. 10:13). Be that as it may, the most well-known term is the one deciphered as a verb "believe," and as a thing "faith." The passages are too numerous, making it impossible to cite or even allude to. The meaning of the word carries with it trust, confidence, repose in one. (See John 3:14-16, 18, 36; Acts 10:43; 13:38-39; 16:31; Rom. 1:16; Gal. 3:26; Eph. 2:8, and many others.).

b. The other aspect of faith that necessities stressing is that in faith one submits to Christ as Lord. In a same act in which we receive him as Savior, we offer ourselves to him as Lord. We become his servants by virtue of the fact that he saves us from sin. Jesus emphasizes this in relation to his followers. The very term disciple suggests that we progress toward becoming students in his school.

We go under his power as teacher. This is the reason Jesus says we should move toward becoming as little children and have the spirit of humility (Matt. 18:1-4). Jesus emphasized this childlike humility in contrast to the spirit of pride and selfishness that desired the best place for self in the kingdom. A same thought is brought out clearly in Matthew 11:25-30.

Here Jesus thanks the Father that reality has been hidden from the wise and prudent, the proud and self-sufficient in spirit, but that he has revealed it unto babes, the those who are humble and open to instruction (teachable). Jesus says that none can know the Father aside from those to whom the Son wills to reveal him. Hence, if a man would know God, he should enter the school of Christ, take his burden, submit to his power, have the spirit of meekness after the supreme example of Jesus himself.

The demand for supreme authority in our lives turns out in those passages where he says that he should come in front of father, mother, brother, sister, wife, house, or lands, even of life itself (Matt. 10:34 ff.; Luke 14:26); likewise in the passage where he says that one can't be his disciple except if he forsakes all (Luke 14:33); where he requests of the rich youthful ruler that he offer all and follow him (Matt. 10:21); where he refuses to enable one to return to cover the dead or say goodbye to his friends and family (Luke 9:57-62); where he makes the acknowledgment of one before the Father to depend upon the confession of him by that one before men (Matt. 10:32-33); where he teaches that obedience to his teaching is the strong, solid foundation for character and destiny (Matt. 7:24-27); where he claims that he as judge will be the arbiter of the final destinies of men (Matt. 25:31 ff.).

So we see that even in the Synoptic Gospels Christ presents himself as absolute Lord of conscience and of life, calling for self-surrender on our part.

In John's Gospel, we locate a same truth. Jesus is one with the Father (10:30), the way, truth, and the life (14:6), the bread of life (6:35), the light of the world (8:12; 9:5), the true vine of which his disciples are branches (15:1 ff.), the good shepherd who gives his life for the sheep (10:11), the mediator of creation (1:3), the life of the world (1:4), the eternal Son of God (1:18).

To put it plainly, every one of the conclusions of the soul are found in him. To believe on him isn't to be condemned (3:18), to have eternal life (3:36); not to believe on him is to be condemned, to have God's wrath abide on us.

Paul discusses the obedience of faith (Rom. 1:5). This may mean the obedience that grows out of faith, or it might mean the obedience that is identical with faith. Whichever construction is put upon it, it is certain that Christian faith has at its heart submission to Christ as Lord. In Romans, chapter six, he shows that a Christian is one who has become into the servant of righteousness (v. 18). Paul and Peter discuss obeying the gospel (II Thess. 1:8; I Peter 4:17). This isn't submission to baptism, but submission to the Christ who is presented in the gospel as Savior and Lord.

An Objection To Christian Faith

Here is where the modern objection to Christianity winds up most keen. This protest, nonetheless, does not normally expect the appearance of a complaint. It generally shows up in the guise of a clarification that devitalizes claims the name of Christ and praises him as the colossal religious pioneer and saint, yet questions making him Lord and still, small voice and of life.

For the sake of flexibility and the self-governance of individual life, objection is made to what the dissident thinks about a contemptible surrender of one's inner voice and will to another. Such a surrender, it is claimed, would devastate our freedom and degraded our personality.

Be that as it may, in actuality, the individuals who assume this attitude of surrender toward Christ don't discover their identities degraded, their wills weakened, or their freedom lost. They find, then again, that their wills are set free and that they are given a power over themselves and their environment and particularly over moral evil that they never knew and by and large that they never envisioned conceivable.

It is this freedom in the gospel that Paul asks the Galatians that they should not surrender but rather contend for (Gal. 5:1 KJV). The point to recall here, be that as it may, is that this freedom comes just by a faith that makes one the eager, willing slave of Jesus Christ. This is one of the Catch 22s of the gospel for which rationale outfits no clarification; it is seen just when experienced. As an issue of experience, in any case, it is as clear and unmistakable (definite) as the experience of vision or hearing.

Man conceives that his first need is opportunity. His first need is a master. Freedom comes just by submission to Jesus Christ as rightful Lord. Anything shy of this attitude of trust and love toward Jesus Christ misses the mark concerning Christian faith. In Ephesians, chapter five, Paul utilizes the outlines of a husband and wife to set forward the relation between Christ and the church.

Once in a while a woman objects in the name of freedom to being subject to a husband. But, it is only in subjection to the lordship of affection that the genuine woman finds the satisfaction of her womanly nature and the acknowledgment of her typical desires.

Obviously, the domination of the spouse by brute force with respect to the husband is a degradation of her personality. In any case, this isn't the sort of subjection that Paul discusses as the divine ideal for the marriage relation. Nor is the lordship of Christ in the Christian's life the domination of force; it is the mastery of the soul by the love of God embodied in Christ and realized by faith in him. It is a mastery that sets one free from the dominion of sin-set him free, not to be a law unto himself, not to divert from all ethical limitation and authority and be a spiritual anarchist in the kingdom of God, but sets him free to serve God.

There is a certain type of mind, pleasing to call itself "modern," that is captivated by the possibility of independence in the moral and spiritual life. This kind of mind imagines that for the soul to be free, all external authority must be rejected. In any case, the decision here is definitely not a decision between the authority of Christ and freedom; it is a choice between the authority of Christ that brings freedom and the domain of sin.

The power of Christ is the only power that can set the soul free from the dominion of sin. This he does by subduing the soul by the power of his redeeming grace. In any case, this grace becomes operative in the soul only as the soul is mastered by it. The domain of sin from which the soul needs to be delivered does not really take the form as sensuality; it might be simply the self-centered life just discussed that denies in principle its dependence for the truth on any power or person outside itself, especially any Person above the realm to which it belongs.

In any case, the self-centered life is a sinful life, regardless of whether it shows itself in the form of sensuality or as scholarly and moral pride that denies one's dependence on rightful authority.

It was this sort of spirit that Jesus rebuked in the urban areas of his day and that called out his great saying in Matthew 11:25 ff., in which he commends the childlike spirit and shows the need of possessing that spirit if one would know the truth and have spiritual rest.

It was this same spirit that makes the cross of Christ and his spiritual authority over the soul of man both a stumbling block and foolishness to some "cutting edge" minds (modern minds). It was this spirit that, while gladly marching its submission to the authority of the law, desired to make a show of the flesh and win its own salvation by keeping the law rather than of accept the good news (the gospel) of the grace of God.

Why Salvation Is Conditioned Upon Faith

Paul says that justification is by faith that it may according to grace. Faith and grace are correlative thoughts (Rom. 4:16). Each infers the other. In the event that salvation is to be of grace on God's part, it must be by faith on man's part. Salvation by grace implies salvation as a free gift on God's part. Be that as it may, God can't give except as a man receives. Receiving salvation as an unmerited gift (or unmerited favor) on God's part is faith. God gives salvation, man receives.

Contradicted to Paul's concept of salvation by grace through faith was the doctrine of salvation by works; that is, that man by his obedience to the law was to merit or deserve salvation. Paul strenuously restricted (opposed) this on the ground that it would totally pervert the gospel.

At the point when Judaizers demanded that Gentiles who accepted the gospel should also be circumcised and keep the law, Paul objected, holding that faith in Christ was sufficient to save. He said this would make salvation a matter of debt on God's part rather than a matter of grace (Rom. 4:4 KJV).

There are, at that point, no conditions of salvation that have been prescribed in any arbitrary way. The only conditions are the conditions that are necessarily involved in the relations of a God of mercy who would, as a matter of grace, save an undeserving sinner to the sinner that he would save. The ethical or moral relations for the case make it impossible for God to save the sinner who does not recognize and acknowledge his sinful condition and cast himself in his helplessness upon a God of grace.

In other words, God can't save a sinner without faith on the sinner's part. In this sense, repentance and faith are not conditions of salvation; they rather constitute salvation; that is, saving a sinner means to bring him to that state of mind in which he denies sin and trusts himself to a God of grace.

As the necessary moral relations involved in the case, repentance and faith are the universal and invariable conditions of salvation. Or on the other hand utilizing faith as including repentance, we may state that faith and faith alone is the condition of salvation. God himself couldn't save the sinner without faith on the sinner's part. To state that he could is say that God saved a man without saving him.

It follows, then, that the conditions of salvation have never changed. To state that some men were saved in one age of the world on one set of conditions, and other men in another age of the world on another set of conditions is to make God a arbitrary God. It is gibberish, non-sense to state that men were saved in Old Testament times by the law and in New Testament times by the gospel. Not one man was ever saved by law, in light of the fact that no man could keep its requirements. (See Acts 13:39; Rom. 7:10 ff.) To state that men were saved by the law would make void the good news of the gospel of the grace of God. Men were saved in Old Testament times same as they are in New Testament times, by faith in God and his promises of grace. (See Romans 4).

It will be promptly seen that this prohibits submersion or some other service of ritual, as a state of salvation. Paul regards that the gospel is the power of God unto salvation (Rom. 1:16 KJV). He plainly recognizes preaching the gospel and baptizing, in a way that would have been impossible, if he had thought of baptism as an essential to the enjoyment of salvation through the gospel (I Cor. 1:14-17 KJV).

Then again, Paul views baptism as symbolical of a salvation procured by faith (Rom. 6:1-4 ASV). The declaration of Peter about being baptized into remission of sins (Acts 2:38 ASV) can be explained in the same way; that is, that baptism symbolizes our passage into a state of remission of sins.

John 3:5 most likely does not allude to baptism by any means, but rather to the cleansing from sin in the new birth, of which baptism is the symbol. In Acts 22:16 ASV, Ananias told Paul to rise and be baptized and wash away his sins. This can be taken either literally, after the manner of the Roman Catholic Church, or symbolically, as Baptists do.

Between these two positions there is no standing ground completely in rationale or in Scripture. The Catholic position totally perverts the whole gospel order and denies the doctrine of salvation by grace. So does any other position that makes man's salvation from sin depend on baptism or anything else than faith in the crucified and risen Redeemer.

Yet, someone may state that, since faith is the sinner's act and since faith is the condition of salvation, after all the sinner's salvation relies upon something that the sinner himself does. Also, since the sinner's salvation is to rely upon something that the sinner does, for what reason would it be advisable for it to not rely upon baptism a condition of salvation as well as on faith? The answer is, that in the sense that this question implies, God did not make faith a condition of salvation.

As officially brought up, confidence isn't a arbitrarily delegated condition of salvation. Faith is the condition of salvation, in light of the fact that the moral relations of the case demand faith.

The grace of God that gives salvation must be appropriated by man's faith. Otherwise grace is in vain. In any case, any act not necessarily involved not with the moral relations of the case, if made a condition of salvation, would be an arbitrary prescription on God's part.

In addition, faith as a state of salvation isn't a act by which man merits or earns anything. It is the act by which the bankrupt sinner receives the grace of God. It is a act in which the sinner puts all his trust for salvation in another and in what that other has done for him. It's anything but an act in which the sinner makes any claim for himself; it is fairly a act in which he recognizes that he can't help himself and in which he transfers ownership of his life to Another.

So there is rather an act of faith in which he acknowledges that he cannot do anything to help himself and by which one signs away his life to Another. It is an act in which one recognizes the utter impossibility of doing this and by which one throws himself on Christ and what he has done for his acceptance with God.

The Relation Of Faith To A Life Of Righteousness

The objection is here and there made to the doctrine of salvation by grace through faith that it would urge one to carry on with a life of spiritual case and sin as opposed to one of acts of kindness and righteous nature. This has been a standing objection since the times of Paul. He has foreseen this objection in his letter to the Romans.

Certainly he had gone over it ordinarily in his content with the Judaizers. Paul shows that a Christian is one who has died to sin and been made alive to uprightness by faith in Christ (Rom. 6:1-4 KJV). This establishes an ethical assurance (the main sort of certification that will apply for the situation) that the Christian will carry on with a life of righteous nature. It is morally inconceivable for him to do whatever else.

It is now and then felt that James and Paul don't agree on this inquiry. Paul says that one is justified by faith apart from works of law (Rom. 3:28 KJV). James says that a man is justified by works and not only by faith (James 2:24). In any case, we should recollect two contrasts in perspective among Paul and James.

One is that they are utilizing the term works in to some degree distinctive faculties. Paul is discussing legalistic works-fills in as a reason for justifying the support or favor of God. What's more, Paul's view was that as a reason for a sinner's acceptance with God, works of law were totally useless.

James is discussing fills in as the outgrowth and expression of a living faith. Once more, Paul's inquiry was: Upon what condition is a sinner justified before God? His answer is: Upon condition of faith, not on condition of works as an meritorious basis. James' inquiry was: What kind of faith is it that justifies? Is it faith that produces good works, acts of kindness, or faith that repeats only a formal statement of faith? His answer is that faith that produces no works is a dead faith, and he contends that this kind of faith won't save (James 2:14 KJV).

Most likely Paul would have embraced James' contention, and James would have concurred with Paul. There is no inconsistency or contradiction except if one demands taking the author's words apart from their connection and without reference to the author's intention. All things considered dialect has no importance whatever.

It isn't true that salvation by faith urges one to a life of transgression (sin) and demoralizes a life of righteous nature. Then again, faith in Christ as Savior from sin is the only thing that will lift one out of a self-centered life. The doctrine of salvation by works prompts a self-centered life. In any case, in the act of faith one looks past self; he confides in another.

He surrenders himself to another. Additionally, faith joins to Christ and his Spirit turns into the controlling power of the Christian's life. As Christ gave himself for us, so the individuals who follow him will offer themselves to him and to the service of their fellows. Gratitude to God for a salvation receive as the gift of his grace won't let one live for self while the world is dying for what he can give.

Chapter Ten

The Consciousness Of Salvation

ONE OF THE EXCEPTIONAL things that about salvation in the Christian sense of the term is that it is a conscious transaction. This was assumed in the sum total of what that has been said in regards to salvation, however it is well presently to give special consideration to it.

The Normal Christian Experience

The typical Christian experience is one in which the Christian has cognizant acceptance with God. The whole religious environment appears to change with the coming of Jesus Christ. Old Testament holy people had cognizant fellowship with God, however they didn't have that full note of happiness, joy and trust in their confidence with God that we find in the New Testament.

Particularly is it true from Pentecost on that men had this full assurance of acceptance with

God. Forgiveness of sins was no merely outer transaction that the forgiven sinner may happen to hear about or not.

1. In any case, there was the awareness of sin

This was delivered by the proclaiming of the gospel. The man who had no awareness or conscious of sin and in whom it couldn't be produced by the word of God was miserably hopeless. The greater sinner isn't in every case more conscious of his sins, yet the more one is conscious of sin, the more is he liable to celebrate or rejoice in salvation and love the God who forgives in mercy (Luke 7:14 ff.).

2. Salvation from sin was a transaction in which one was carried into cognizant fellowship with God.

In this exchange one discovers God. He comes to know God (John 17:3 KJV). God comes to possess man and man to possess God. He will be their God and they will be his people (Heb. 8:10). In a genuine sense a man has no God until the point that he comes to possess him in this incredible revolutionary crisis of life.

In this emergency a covenant is sealed by which the soul becomes deliberately offered over to him. At the point when sin was removed and the soul came into fellowship with God, the soul was frequently overflowed with joy. (See Acts 8:8; 13:52 KJV). The justified man had a legacy of peace to which he was entitled by virtue of his new relation with God (Rom. 5:1 KJV).

Another element that comes because of this fellowship with God in Christ was trust. New Testament Christians were forward looking (Rom. 8:24).

This does not imply that Christian experiences were alike then any more than they are currently. Some were more enthusiastic and calamitous than others. Lydia did not appear to have the unsettling of soul that the prison guard had (Jailer) (Acts 16). Nor does it imply that one must have the capacity to return in memory to the exact time when he had an experience of salvation. There are assortments of Christian experience, just as there are differences among men in each other respect.

In any case, every normal Christian experience is an experience of conscious acceptance with God in the forgiving of sins, an experience that brings love, happiness, joy, peace, and hope to the soul.

The Lack Of Assurance

However it must be perceived that there are instances of the individuals who have been recovered who don't have clear and unmistakable cognizance of acknowledgment with God. This is perceived in the New Testament and is confirmed in Christian experience. John says that he composed his Gospel that men may have life by putting stock in Jesus as the Christ (20:31). He says that he composed the First Epistle all together that the individuals who accept may realize that they have everlasting life (5:13).

This plainly suggests two things. One is that it is the benefit of a spared man to realize that he is spared. The other is that a man might be spared and not have this affirmation. On the off chance that salvation and confirmation were indivisible, at that point John's composition of the Epistle was futile; he was all things considered written work to convey to Christians something that they couldn't be Christians and not have.

In some cases assurance is inadequate in the beginning of the Christian life; in some cases one may have it and lose it. Now and then the lack of assurance is caused by sin and disobedience in the life; in some cases it is because of an absence of comprehension of a portion of the fundamental and elemental things in the Christian life, for example, the ground of our forgiveness in the redeeming work of Christ, of faith as the essential and all-inclusive condition of salvation.

Now and again, the absence of assurance is caused by the fact that one didn't get only the sort of experience he was searching for. A few people need the sort of religious experience Paul had, and, along these lines, are continually dissatisfied with the one God has given them. In still other cases, lack of assurance is because of scholarly perplexities. One might be bothered in light of the fact that he can't work out his own satisfaction all of the issues concerning God and his dealings with man.

What Is Necessary To Assurance

A Word may be said now about how assurance is produced or what is important to assurance.

In any case, one needs a reasonable comprehension and a firm handle of the essential things in salvation. It is not necessarily the case that he should be a specialist scholar or theologian.

He doesn't. Nor is it to state with the Catholic beliefs that, if he doesn't trust certain authoritative opinions, he will be hellish cursedness. In any case, he needs a firm handle on the way that Christ has made full provision for our sins and that we are saved by faith in Jesus.

There can be no definite assurance of salvation where one doesn't get a handle on this reality. Some of the time one may realize that he has been changed without having a clear awareness of salvation, but this reasonable cognizance of salvation will come when one immovably gets a handle on the way that it is faith in the crucified and risen Redeemer that saves. Alongside this there must be definite surrender to Christ as Lord. The will must surrender to him. There must be no cognizant and stiff-necked disobedience to Christ.

Assembling what has been stated, it will be seen that the total of it is that one must have clear and definite faith to have assurance of acceptance with God. Faith brings its own assurance; and only faith is necessary.

Dr. A. H. Strong (2014) says: "The ground of faith (which means saving faith) is the eternal word of promise. The ground of assurance, then again, is the internal witness of the Spirit that we fulfill the conditions of the promise." This statement is to some degree deceiving. It establishes the impression that the ground of saving faith is a certain something, and that the ground of the faith that brings assurance is something else. In any case, this is a mistake. The faith that saves is the faith that assures.

Saving faith conveys its own assurance, and, in the event that it doesn't, it is on account of the faith isn't clear and definite. If one needs assurance, he won't get it by having developed in him a new kind of faith or faith in a different object. Assurance will come when faith is clarified, fortified, and mindful of what it is about. Jesus Christ is always the object of faith, and the Holy Spirit is the power that produces faith in Christ.

This is true both in salvation and assurance. At the end of the day, Christ and the Holy Spirit both bear the same relation to saving faith that they do in assuring faith, for these are one faith, not two.

These are called attention to in the New Testament certain moral and spiritual qualities that mark the regenerated man. Some of these are the ownership of the Spirit (Rom. 8:9, 14; I John

3:24 KJV), obedience to Christ or God (John 14:15, 21; I John 2:34), an life of righteousness and of victory over sin (I John 3:6-9), love of the brotherhood (I John 3:10 ff.), the power to discern the truth (I John 2:27).

These are all the results of our faith in Jesus Christ. When we are asked to take a look at these as evidences of regeneration, we are basically asked to let our faith become clear and self-conscious and realize what it is about. We are not asked to take something outside of or beyond saving faith as evidence of our salvation.

Bibliography

Beecher, W. J. (2002) The Prophets And The Promise. Eugene. Or.: Wipf & Stock Publisher

Caird, G. B. (1994, 1995) New Testament Theology. Oxford, UK.: New York, NY.: Oxford University Press, Clarendon Press

Ferre, N. F. S. (1942) The Christian Faith. New York, NY.: London, UK.: Harper And Brothers

Flew, R. N. (1943) Jesus And His Church. New York, NY.: Abingdon Press

Forsythe, P. T. (2010) Christian Perfection. London, Eng.: Wales.: Bibliobazar, Forgotten Books, Hodder & Stoughton

James, W. (2016) Varieties Of Religious Experience. Edinburgh, Scotland.: Trinity Press

Mullins, E. Y. (2012) The Christian Religion In It's Doctrinal Expression (reprint) London, ENG.: Mishawaka, IN.: Judson Press, Forgotten Books

Schelermacher (2011) The Christian Faith. New York, NY.: London, UK.: T&T Clark LTD

Strong, A. H. (2014) Systematic Theology, Vols. 1-3. USA.: CreateSpace Independent Publishing Platform

The Holy Bible (1964) Authorized King James Version. Chicago, Ill.: J. G. Ferguson

The Holy Bible (1953) The Revised Standard Version. Nashville, TN.: Thomas Nelson & Sons (Used By Permission)

The Holy Bible (1901) The American Standard Version. Nashville, TN.: Thomas Nelson (Used By Permission)

The Holy Bible (1959) The Berkeley Version. Grand Rapids, MI.: Zondervan (Used By Permission)

About The Author

THE REVEREND DR. JOHN Thomas Wylie is one who has dedicated his life to the work of God's Service, the service of others; and being a powerful witness for the Gospel of Our Lord and Savior Jesus Christ. Dr. Wylie was called into the Gospel Ministry June 1979, whereby in that same year he entered The American Baptist College of the American Baptist Theological Seminary, Nashville, Tennessee.

As a young Seminarian, he read every book available to him that would help him better his understanding of God as well as God's plan of Salvation and the Christian Faith. He made a commitment as a promising student that he would inspire others as God inspires him. He understood early in his ministry that we live in times where people question not only who God is; but whether miracles are real, whether or not man can make a change, and who the enemy is or if the enemy truly exists.

Dr. Wylie carried out his commitment to God, which has been one of excellence which led to his earning his Bachelors of Arts in Bible/Theology/Pastoral Studies. Faithful and obedient to the call of God, he continued to matriculate in his studies earning his Masters of Ministry from Emmanuel Bible College, Nashville, Tennessee & Emmanuel Bible College, Rossville, Georgia. Still, inspired to please the Lord and do that which is well – pleasing in the Lord's sight, Dr. Wylie recently on March 2006, completed his Masters of Education degree with a concentration in Instructional Technology earned at The American Intercontinental University, Holloman Estates, Illinois. Dr. Wylie also previous to this, earned his Education Specialist Degree from Jones International University, Centennial, Colorado and his Doctorate of Theology from The Holy Trinity College and Seminary, St. Petersburg, Florida.

Dr. Wylie has served in the capacity of pastor at two congregations in Middle Tennessee and Southern Tennessee, as well as served as an Evangelistic Preacher, Teacher, Chaplain, Christian Educator, and finally a published author, writer of many great inspirational Christian Publications such as his first publication: *"Only*

One God: Who Is He?" – published August 2002 via formally 1st books library (which is now AuthorHouse Book Publishers located in Bloomington, Indiana & Milton Keynes, United Kingdom) which caught the attention of *The Atlanta Journal Constitution Newspaper.*

Dr. Wylie is happily married to Angel G. Wylie, a retired Dekalb Elementary School teacher who loves to work with the very young children and who always encourages her husband to move forward in the Name of Jesus Christ. They have Four children, 11 grand-children and one great-grandson of whom they are very proud. Both Dr. Wylie and Angela Wylie serve as members of the Salem Baptist Church, located in Lilburn, Georgia, where the Reverend Dr. Richard B. Haynes is Senior pastor.

Dr. Wylie has stated of his wife: "she knows the charm and beauty of sincerity, goodness, and purity through Jesus Christ. Yes, she is a Christian and realizes the true meaning of loveliness as the reflection as her life of holy living gives new meaning, hope, and purpose to that of her husband, her children, others may say of her, "Behold the handmaiden of the Lord." A Servant of Jesus Christ!

About The Book

IN THIS PUBLICATION, "A Doctrine On The Beginning Of The Christian Faith," It points to the fact that God is working out through Jesus Christ and his Church a redemptive program on the earth. Redemption is to be the goal and peak of creation. There is nothing more profound in the mind and purpose behind God than his plan to redeem. God works out his redemption regardless of the restricting powers on the earth.

The Bible says, "With wicked hands men crucified him, in doing so they carried out what was in the determinate counsel and foreknowledge of God" (Acts 2:23). Jesus was crucified on our behalf. This is his redemptive work as it works itself out in human experience.

What is becoming a Christian? What sort of a transaction is it? What do we mean by salvation? How is a man saved?

These questions strike a chord when we think about them from the point of view of involvement and life. Is salvation something that takes place all at once or is it a continuous process?

"The Son of man came to seek and to save that which was lost" (Luke 19:10). Faithful is the saying, and worthy of all acceptation, that Christ Jesus came into the world to save sinners" (I Timothy 1:15).

"For God so loved the world, that he gave his only begotten Son, that whosoever believeth in him should not perish, but have everlasting life" (John 3:16). "For God sent not his Son into the world to condemn the world; but that the world through him might be saved" (John 3:17).

"He that believeth on him is not condemned; but he that believeth not is condemned already because he hath believed in the name of the only begotten Son of God (Jesus Christ)" (John 3:18).

Reverend Dr. John Thomas Wylie